Mum, Dad and everyone else who has contributed and allowed me to be the best version of myself in writing this, thank you.

And, to the 'Sausages' whose horseplay and antics at university made it that bit better.

4

Teaching Teachers

Published by UK Book Publishing

www.ukbookpublishing.com

ISBN: 978-1-917329-03-3

5

Prologue

I have created this book to teach you what they don't teach you at teaching university. But what do I know? At the time of reading, I can guarantee to you that you probably have more experience teaching than I do. However, in my three years since graduating from an old school traditional teaching college in one of the oldest cities in the United Kingdom, I have come to realise that while you learn a lot in theory, when the spotlights are on you or should I say the projector glare is on you, and you are in the moment, all of the stuff you have been taught can go out the window. In that moment, you don't think of Bloom's Taxonomy; you think, 'what the....'.

Hopefully, by reading this book, you can use the experiences that I and other fellow teachers have learned to gain insight into making our job as educators that little bit easier, be it your first year out or you're beginning to think about hanging up the elbow patches. This book is not a replacement for formal education, but rather a supplement to it. It is a resource to help you navigate the challenges that come with being a teacher, sharing practical tips and tricks that can only be learned through experience. While some of this book may seem obvious to some, I hope that it can serve everyone at least once in their career. So, let's dive in and learn together.

Registration

Chapter 1

'There is no safety net'- Mr J

At the age of twenty-one, I realised that for the first time in my life, I was alone, I was by myself, and most daunting of all, I was in charge. Sure, being in charge of two dozen eggs doesn't seem that bad, but to be in charge of two dozen thirteen-year-olds, on your first official day of teaching- that is a reality check for you.

Up until that point, there has always been someone else with the answers, as children we look up to our mums, dads, grandparents, even our teachers- they become these deities that just seem to know everything and keep us on the right side of life. When life seemed to be getting tough (tough in the context of a child anyway), it was the adults around us who had the answers. From infancy up to graduation, you have these people who are there looking out for you- and then, no one.

I don't think it ever crossed my mind that I was now one of these deities that children now look to for the answers– that's a daunting reality to conclude with when you have twenty-four pairs of eyes staring at you on your first day of teaching, ever.

Picture the scene, you've just had a week in sun-splitting August of meetings about pupils, departments, and school policies, surrounded by people who seem to have their act together. Aside from a brief introduction to you at the start of the first meeting on the first day, these people hardly know you exist. They are here to do their job and have their people around them. It's hard to imagine where a baby teacher fits into all of that.

If that wasn't enough, after a week of tedium and information overload, they handed you your timetable. You realise that you have 5 KS3 classes, a GCSE and maybe even an A level, all maxed to capacity with children. That's a lot of new names. But even then, I don't think reality hits.

It will only hit, period one, Monday morning, your first class. At that precise moment, you realise that there isn't another teacher sitting in the store beside you with a cup of coffee like there was on teaching practice. You realise that there isn't an inspector at the back of the room with a pen and paper watching your every move. In that moment, it dawns on you, this is YOUR classroom, YOUR class, YOUR responsibility.

Now that is daunting. It would be easy to get overwhelmed in that scenario, you think how on earth can you do it? How on earth can you, a twenty-one-year-old be in charge of people who aren't that much younger than you? How can you possibly live up to the same standard and mythology of the adults in my life when I was that age? You wouldn't be human if you didn't get intimidated by that, there isn't a teacher on this earth who hasn't gotten intimated by children at some point.

Hope is not lost however, because as you settle into it, and period one turns into two and week one turns into week two, you start to get a bit more confident, and you start to realise that what you were so scared of, being in charge, isn't all that bad in the grand scheme of things. Yes, it gives you higher levels of stress, anxiety, and worry, but it also gives you, freedom.

Just like the first time you drive a car by yourself after you pass your driving test, you realise you have the freedom, to do what you want– to an extent, of course. You can teach in the way that you are comfortable, teach in a way that you think the children in your school will understand, teach in a way that will allow you, to be you– not this idealistic version of yourself that the university has told you, you have to be.

Don't get me wrong, you are still very much governed by codes of practice and conduct policies– but you realise after the initial fear of teaching by yourself, that you are teaching... by yourself– and that is exhilarating.

Chapter 2

'It's not as glamorous as people say'- Mrs B

My granny, to this day will talk about her teachers. 'Mr C' was her favourite for sure. She would reminisce about how when he walked down the corridors, the children would move out of the way in his presence, how he was a figure head in society, and he commanded respect from everyone he met.

'Mr I', by far was my favourite at school. At the time I was failing the subject that I would later go on to teach, I had no heart in it. My teacher didn't seem to care, he was retiring, and I was just unfortunate enough to be his last A level class. After he left, 'Mr I' appeared, he immediately pulled the place together and set us on the right path again. He motivated me and kept me going pushing through the two years and I eventually came out with not only a passing result, but one good enough to get into university with.

He allowed me to have a future doing something that I enjoyed, and ultimately just got lost in the lack of momentum and attention given by his predecessor. For that I will forever be grateful and look up to him for doing, he is arguably the person I try to model myself on as an educator.

For generations teachers have been viewed as the old guard. One of the last professions and ultimately people who are someone in society. Or so I thought, I'd be lying if I said that I thought this was true for the entire generation, purely because it is what I thought.

Sadly though, actually starting out my career as a teacher, I've come to realise that teaching is viewed slightly differently in today's society comparing to how it actually is. People see our holidays, our six-hour workdays and our every weekend off as enough of a reason to become a teacher. Sadly though, for many, it's not enough to become, or stay as a teacher.

Teaching is tough, you don't check out at the last bell in the day, your work comes home with you, and yes you have every weekend off, but chances are you are spending that time planning for the week ahead.

There is a perception that teaching is easy, unconfrontational and almost part time because of the holidays, I can confirm– it's not. You do not stop as a teacher, you are constantly preparing resources, planning lessons, or even replaying the day's events in your head.

Even as recently as last Christmas, I went out with some university mates, the talk wasn't about what Santa brought– more what our schools did. We recalled events about what had happened from the last time we had met up, our stories, while similar and relatable were more a method of venting of our grievances. When we had finally exhausted our back catalogue, the next person went. This went on for the rest of the night, into the wee hours we talked about people X, Y and Z who were roadblocks in our peaceful living of being a teacher.

It's not to say teaching is a career path you should stay away from– by no means. If anything, I would encourage someone to become a teacher. The reward from watching a pupil's eyes widening as he or she finally understand a topic is like no other feeling. There is a sense of community within a school setting that is something like no other, there's a sense of comradery for sure. However, I do think those considering a venture in education should be very aware of the challenges that comes with it. Yes, all jobs are challenging, such as life, but as a teacher, it certainly will test you.

There will be pupils that will push, mentally, and some maybe even physically too! There will be days where you don't leave until the caretaker kicks you out. There will be occasions where you think, 'why?!'. But, equally as so, there will be pupils who are a pleasure to teacher, you will have favourites, and you will look forward to those classes coming each week. There will be times, where you are proud of the work you have done, how staying late was worth the effort for the end result. And there will be times where you do ask yourself, 'why?' but then you remember about the thousands of children in your career that you have been able to help and have your own fingerprint on their formation into adulthood, the lasting legacy you leave on your pupils, will likely outlast you.

While teaching isn't everything that society has viewed it to be, certainly not within the last twenty years anyway, and while it is very challenging for young and experienced teachers alike– it is still one of the most rewarding careers out there, it is still one of the most fulfilling careers out there, and it is still one of the careers that will allow you to have a lasting impression on all of the pupils you are fortunate enough to teach.

Now, if only we can get the pay up a bit!

Chapter 3

'It doesn't pay you'- Mr M

At the time of writing this, teachers are about to strike for the second time this academic year. The reason you ask? The reason why valuable education is getting interrupted from primary one to fourth year undergraduate level? Pay.

Don't get me wrong, as someone who worked a part time job during university, the pay increase from minimum wage, sixteen hours a week to M1 level pay, was noticeable. But just, noticeable. As a newly qualified university graduate teacher, you end up making annually, just slightly more than someone who works a 40-hour week, minimum wage job with no formal education.

With that in mind, it's easy to see why a large population of newly graduated teachers often get confronted with the realisation that their initial pay packet may not exactly reflect that of their education level and workload, resulting in them leaving the profession for pastures greener or should I say, richer.

It doesn't need said, but the lack of compensation comparing to workload isn't just demoralising, but it can lead to financial strain, and particularly for someone young, looking to set out on that chapter of their life, its near impossible to do so. Especially with all the 12-foot hoops mortgage providers try and have you jump through. You often become frozen in time, where you earn enough to live, but that's just about it.

Despite this, it is important to realise that for initial teachers, just setting out. Teaching is a cumulative process. Not only do you gain more experience the more years you have under your belt, but you gain more earning potential as well. While initially, M1 pay is modest comparing to first year doctors, engineers or even firemen. Those teachers who stick with it, climb through M1, M2, M3 and so on, can earn more, as each year goes on.

However, if you are just desperate to set out and buy that shiny red sports car in your first few years of teaching, you can speed up the process slightly, by earning responsibility points within your school. These points equate to a little bump in your pay packet each month. While it's not enough to allow you to get your backside into some finely tuned Italian horsepower, it might just be enough for that extra tank of petrol!

These points aren't free however, you do have to earn your pay increase each month. Often by taking on available roles within the school, such as Head of Year, Head of Department, Head of timetabling.

While this on paper seems like a good idea, take it from someone who has tried to buy that sports car in their early years of teaching. Sometimes jumping in too quickly by taking on too much can just add to the already stressful day to day life of teaching. Ask yourself before taking on any additional responsibility points, why exactly that point is available to begin with? Why aren't the more experienced teachers applying for it? And what work is involved in it? My recommendation, if it's something that interests you, or seems convenient enough to do in the non-contact time you've been assigned, then go for it. If your school is expecting you to rebuild the entire curriculum structure of the STEM subjects in a 35-minute period, each week- chances are this one can go a miss.

In some schools, you'll find that often, some teachers adopt what I call, the 'Pokemon' approach, simply because, 'they gotta catch them all' when it comes to responsibility points. This, I believe isn't for finical reasoning, more just for the clout that comes with having so many roles and titles. In all schools, if you do accumulate enough points behind your name, you can get invited on to the 'Senior Leadership Team'.

This team, while having the monopoly on responsibility points within the school, it is rightly deserved and financially compensated for, as they also have the monopoly on much of the stress that comes with the title as well.

The important thing to remember when it comes to teachers pay, just like most things, when you stick with it long enough, it will pay off... get it? Pay...

Chapter 4

'You are always learning'- Mr J

As a young teacher, it's easy to fall into the trap of thinking you know everything. You've just graduated, armed with knowledge and enthusiasm, ready to impart wisdom to your students. But the truth is you are still what people in my school would call a 'baby teacher'.

Teaching is a never-ending journey of learning, we as teachers, learn as much as the pupils we have been tasked to teach. It's like being on a rollercoaster, where you're constantly surprised, challenged, and sometimes even thrown for a loop. The best thing to do is to embrace this journey and realise that there's not a single person on this planet who knows everything and...hold on to your keys for dear life.

We all make mistakes, and that's okay. In fact, it's essential for growth, there is not one teacher in your school, my school, or any school for that matter, who hasn't made a mistake or two in their lifetime. Believe you me, I've made enough for two teachers!

When you step into the classroom, you're not just there to teach; you're there to learn as well. Every interaction with your students is an opportunity for growth. You learn from their questions, their perspectives, and even their behaviour, good and bad.

It's a humbling experience to realise that you, as a teacher, are constantly evolving alongside the children you're tasked to educate. In a way its poetic, in a way, its painfully scary.

You may have your lesson planned meticulously, but then a student asks a question that throws you off guard. It's in these moments that you realise the beauty of being a forever learner. You don't have all the answers, and that's perfectly fine. What matters is your willingness to adapt and grow.

In that exact situation, it's simply a matter of saying; 'you know what? I'm not really sure of that answer, can I get back to you on that?', yes this shows the children that we don't know everything, but it also shows them that we are being honest and transparent with them– that's a quality that they will appreciate.

I am a serial planner, on my teaching practise I had my folder colour coordinated with those little sticky arrows, I'm fairly certain I sold out my local shop I had that many on it. I had every lesson planned to within an inch of its life- but planned in an ideal world where nothing can go wrong. I only learnt when teaching in a real school, a school that has snow days, that has football days, that has global pandemic days, that it is important embrace the chaos of the classroom, relish in the unexpected twists and turns of each day and remember that every stumble is just another opportunity to learn something new.

Every teacher has their own experiences, techniques and tips to get them through the day- one thing I regret in my first year of teaching was not going around the more experienced hands and asking them for their pearls of wisdom. As a twenty-one-year-old, you aren't kidding anyone when you walk down the corridors acting as if you own the place, you are not the first and you are not the last.

If I had the opportunity to start again, I'd go around the heads of department relevant to my subjects, I'd go to the teachers with one foot out the door on to the retirement cruise, id even go as far as speaking to the principal, and gaining any small insight I could that could allow me to better myself.

At the end of the day, it is the realisation that every teacher has their own fingerprinted technique when it comes to their practice. That entire concept has inspired me and ultimately informed me to write this book. Teachers of all ages, backgrounds and subjects have contributed to the chapters of this book and while I'm sure there is more than likely going to be something that I have for-sure missed. This is the 'Swiss Army Knife' of teacher's tips and tricks gathered from people who have been around the school playground once or twice in their day.

After all, the best teachers are those who never stop learning and help those to do the same.

Chapter 5

'If you don't know, ask'- Miss K

One Friday evening, the head of examinations called me. At the time I thought 'this is weird, she never calls me'. I answered phone, that was my first mistake... The second mistake came in the form of her telling me that I had accidently entered the wrong exam code for an A level class. As a result, the examining body was asking for coursework that my class simply hadn't completed. After a lengthy pause, she told me to not worry, that she would sort it and that I was to go and enjoy my weekend.

Needless to say, I did not enjoy my weekend. I spent the entirety of that three-day period, worried about what would be waiting for me come Monday morning Thankfully, she did sort it- and it wasn't a problem that didn't have an adequate solution.

However, this is something that could have been easily avoided. In the moment, on the call as she was telling me what exactly I had done- I remember back to send the same woman an email with an exam code for my subject that I just wasn't entirely convinced was the right one, but, because this was my second year of doing it– I thought, 'I can't exactly tell her I don't know, can I?'. I concluded that pride was better than certainty and sent it, despite my doubts. I really wish now that I hadn't sent that email, rather send one asking for a bit of clarity on which code it should be.

The moral of the story is, despite what your ego might be telling you, it is better to be sure rather than sorry. Pride is not an adequate substitution for certainty.

The simple fact of the matter is, no one has all the answers– everyone can be unsure, so much so it is almost expected by more senior teachers to have less experienced teachers come and ask them for advice– such is life. When time moves on, those younger teachers will be more senior and can pass the advice on to the then younger educators, and the wheels keep turning. It's how it works.

On a more fundamental level, how as teachers can we be expected to preach to our pupils; 'if you're not sure ask the person beside you' or 'if you don't know the answer, come and ask rather than getting it wrong', when we don't do it ourselves. Are we that prideful we would rather be hypocritical?

There is no shame in asking for help, if the world didn't ask for help; the United States of America wouldn't have provided the allies with significant military supplies in September 1940 during World War 2- ultimately helping them win the war or even as recently as recently as modern times, where countries around the world helped each other in fighting against the Covid-19 pandemic that swept the entire globe. Imagine what the world would be like if help wasn't given in those two exact moments in time.

Now don't get me wrong, asking for advice or help in a school setting, isn't as a significant moment in modern history as say the end of the bloodiest war in modern history- but it's still something that, any self-respecting teacher, who can self-develop and grow should do.

When seeking advice in a school setting, it's important to approach the situation with respect and consideration. Whether you're seeking academic guidance, personal advice, or help with a particular issue, it is important that you treat every situation with as much respect and decorum as possible, especially when it may concern others in the school.

When asking for advice in a school setting, it's crucial to choose the right person to approach. This could be a teacher, counsellor, or mentor who you trust and feel comfortable speaking with. Consider the individual's expertise and their ability to provide relevant guidance. At the end of the day, while the school counsellor can provide top quality advice about real world problems ongoing in a pastoral setting– they may not be able to appropriately advise on curriculum aspects or problems. In the same way, if you went to a busy head of department, chances are they want to talk shop rather than talk personally– which is obviously understandable given their primary objective within the role is to manage their department to have positive outcomes.

It's also important to remember that when approaching someone for advice, it's essential to be respectful and courteous. Start the conversation with a polite greeting and express your appreciation for their time and willingness to help. If they are already talking to someone, don't just immediately jump into the conversation– wait at a respectable distance and allow them to notice you at a point within a lull in their conversation. It is also worth bearing in mind that given who you are talking to, the initial greeting may also change. The school's principal should absolutely, not be addressed in the same way as of that of the people you take your lunch with.

When the time comes, and you have approached the correct person you are seeking the advice from, make sure to clearly articulate what you need advice on. Whether it's related to academics, personal issues, or career guidance, being specific about your concerns will help the person understand how they can best assist you.

Despite how boring the conversation may then become- and believe you me, it may become very boring if its advice on a particular sub paragraph of page one hundred and whatever of the teaching handbook that was last ratified when televisions were in black and white, you need to remain attentive and focused. When seeking advice, it's important to listen actively to the person's response. Show that you value their input by maintaining eye contact, nodding to indicate understanding, and asking follow-up questions if necessary.

It should go without saying but regardless of the outcome of the conversation, always express gratitude for the person's time and advice. A simple 'thank you' goes a long way in showing appreciation for their support. Believe it or not, in a building full of professional adults, you may be surprised to know that simple messages of thanks, often can go forgotten about.

Depending on the nature of the advice sought, it may be beneficial to follow up with the person at a later time. This demonstrates your commitment to addressing the issue and allows for further discussion or clarification if needed. Not only that, but if the person you have sought the advice from has suggested that they have an input into the situation, such as lending a hand, making a phone call or even looking something up for you, it's a polite way of essentially saying 'remember you said you would do this?'. Often, in this case the helpful colleague genuinely has forgotten to and is still more than willing to help. It's important to exercise professionalism here and not call them out for forgetting. At the end of the day, your request is the bottom of the pile with their day-to-day teaching and roles and responsibility on top of it.

By following these steps, you can effectively ask for advice in a school setting while fostering positive relationships with those who provide guidance. Depending on the severity of the advice, a bar of chocolate would do no harm if it made its way on to their desks as a small token of thanks!

Chapter 6

'You are your own worst critic'- Ms B

I had a brief stint as Head of Year, and while the job was hugely rewarding- one of the things that I disliked the most, was when I was acknowledged in assembly for something that I or I and my year group had done. It's not that I thought that it wasn't deserved, believe you me, I am very proud of all that I achieved in the role, but its more that as teachers we tend to be very harsh on ourselves. We tend to find the negative rather than the positive. So, when the principal would stand in the assembly hall and say some words of encouragement or positivity towards something I had done- I often thought in my head, 'yeah, sure, that attendance is good, but it's not great... yeah sure, that idea I had is working well, but it could work better' or even 'she is just saying that because she has to...'

Teachers are often their own worst critics, as they strive to provide the best possible education and pastoral support for their students, and often our self-critical perspective can be attributed to several factors, including personal expectations, societal pressures, and the nature of the teaching profession.

We are often highly motivated individuals who have a deep passion for education and a strong desire to make a difference in the lives of our students. This passion can lead to high personal expectations, as we strive to be the best version of ourselves and constantly seek ways to improve our teaching methods and techniques. Whether we want to or not, we often take our work home and replay it over in our heads, wondering– if that was the right decision, should I have said that? Or is this something that can be worked on a bit more? In the role, we are never really satisfied. Which on paper is great, we are a perpetual machine that are constantly seeking to improve ourselves, our pupils or our school, but it also means we are never satisfied, never full, never happy. We can pick faults in the one percent of the day we aren't truly happy with, and it eats us alive until the next day comes, the cycle repeats.

Not exclusive to the deep motivation to succeed, we also have large force coming upon us from societal pressures. Society places a great deal of importance on education, and teachers are often seen as the key to a student's success. As a result, teachers feel a tremendous responsibility to ensure their students excel academically and develop essential life skills. This pressure to perform can lead to a self-critical perspective, as teachers constantly evaluate their own performance and look for ways to improve. We as teachers are focused on getting the best possible success out of our pupils– again, this isn't a bad thing, however it is the expectations placed on us from society that allows us to be hyper critical of ourselves and open us up to vulnerability of additional pressures on top of the existing ones we place upon ourselves.

As teachers we are constantly exposed to a variety of students, each with their unique learning styles and needs. This constant variation in the teaching environment can be challenging and can lead teachers to question their own abilities and effectiveness in the classroom. Especially as a young teacher, you come into a school with these idealistic ideas of 'how' to teach. You are taught through your entire career at university that 'this' is how you teach– well in the real world, that's not always the correct way. Every pupil has different learning styles, in the same way they have different fingerprints– each is unique. Some may learn very similarly to that of someone else, but every pupil will have slight differences in their learning style. No two pupils are alike. As a result, you may plan a perfect lesson on anything of any subject, and think it's the dogs dinner, however, often, you find it doesn't quite resonate with everyone in the class, and that's okay! You would be naive to think it would hit with everyone in the class, however it's easy to take that lack of full understanding by every pupil, and translate that to your teaching ability being sub-par.

We have all been there. American football players call it the 'Yips'. A phenomenon where you convince yourself, something has changed. You tell yourself that you suddenly can't do what you were able to do yesterday, the more you tell yourself this, the more it seems to be the case, you fall deeper into it and before you know it, you are doubting if you were ever good at it to begin with.

If this book teaches you nothing else but this, it's important to remember that the 'Yips' is entirely you. As you are going though mental turmoil, telling yourself that you can't do it, that this isn't for you, the rest of the world is looking at you and nothing has changed, nothing will change, they simply see you as capable today as they did yesterday.

It's not all doom and gloom however, teachers' self-critical perspective can lead to a commitment to continuous improvement, as they actively seek out new teaching strategies, resources, and ideas to better serve their students. This dedication to growth and development can result in more effective teaching practices and a more engaging learning environment for students.

On the other hand, the constant self-evaluation and pressure to be perfect can lead to burnout and stress among teachers. The feeling of never being good enough can be emotionally draining, and the continuous search for improvement can be exhausting.

While it is important for teachers to maintain a critical perspective of their own performance to continually improve, it is also important for them to recognise their accomplishments and maintain a healthy balance. We need to ensure that we find a middle ground by fostering a more balanced perspective.

Chapter 7

'Perspective is key'- Ms B

Potato, potato, same thing, right? Despite that fact those words are literally the same, I can near enough guarantee to you that despite that, you still read them, each with a different affliction and a different perspective.

The title of this chapter speaks for itself really, perspective is key. I have come to understand the significance of perspective in the educational setting. Working in a school environment has taught me that my own personal outlook and perspective can greatly influence interactions with students, colleagues, and parents. Which in turn, can either make life very difficult or not.

One of the most crucial aspects of teaching is understanding the perspectives of students. Each student comes from a unique background and possesses individual experiences that shape their worldview. As much as we can have information on each child to do with a manner of different things, it is impossible to know exactly how that child is tuned to see the world. Some pupils may appear to be having to the same outlook as their peers, however often or not, they are very dissimilar, and each child is uniquely different. As teachers, it is essential to acknowledge and respect these differences in perspective. By doing so, educators can create an inclusive and supportive learning environment where every student feels valued. This is key, to harvesting a thriving learning environment which yields results– if teachers cannot do this, it often can lead to issues beyond the educational setting within the classroom, where it simply does not work. As young teachers, it is easy to fall into the trap of bringing divisive issues into the classroom, there is simply no place for that and will also neglect the perspective of one or more individual pupils. Its best to avoid where possible.

In today's multicultural and diverse classrooms, embracing various perspectives is vital. Teachers must recognise the value of diversity and incorporate diverse perspectives into their teaching practices. This not only enriches the educational experience but also fosters empathy and understanding among students. It allows teachers to become relatable and approachable in the perspective of pupils who they interact with. This not only makes for a more inclusive and engaging learning environment but also makes the teachers life a lot easier.

Perspective extends beyond the student-teacher dynamic and encompasses interactions with colleagues as well. Collaborating with fellow educators provides an opportunity to gain new perspectives, share best practices, and collectively work towards enhancing the learning environment. By valuing diverse perspectives within the staff, teachers can cultivate a more cohesive and supportive professional community. Many schools, have a range of teachers who come from different backgrounds, be it geographical locations, religious beliefs or varying morals. In my own school, central in the country, we have teachers from as near as across the street from the school but as far as over an hour and a half away, as a result, we all come from different backgrounds. While this paints a rich tapestry of stories, experiences and perspectives, that as a young teacher you can absorb like a sponge, it also creates a minefield of problems. It is important to ensure that you remain professional when talking to your colleagues and being mindful that your beliefs, values and morals may be different to the person you are interacting with and has no place inside of the school gates.

By all means, build relationships with those you work with, have best friends or even find the love of your life, but be very mindful that first and foremost you have to work together with these people, and as a result, you should be mindful of sharing divisive opinions.

Another aspect where perspective plays a pivotal role is in engaging with parents and guardians. Understanding the perspectives of families can lead to more effective communication and collaboration. At university, you are taught to adopt almost a 'the customer is always right' mindset and treat the parent with kid gloves and allow them to believe they are always right. However, this is not always the case, and a difficult conversation may be needed. I recall, one occasion, about two weeks into being the head of year nine, where a parent came in with the belief that their child was right, in a situation, where they simply weren't. When the parent was made aware of this, they went cataclysmic and was beyond the point of reasoning, in that moment, we do have to be mindful that you have just challenged their perspective of their child, however we do not have to tolerate disrespect. Afterall, respect is very much a two-way street, while I didn't stoop to the level of the parent by retaliating in such a similar way, I did however remind the parent that if we are able to come to an appropriate solution, we would need to be on the same perspective as for what is to come next. When teachers take the time to empathise with parental viewpoints, it strengthens the home-school partnership, ultimately benefiting the students, however, it is important to remember that respect goes both ways.

Perspective also influences teaching strategies. Recognising that students have different learning styles and preferences requires teachers to adapt their methods to accommodate diverse perspectives. By being flexible in approach, educators can better cater to the individual needs of their students. It's important to bear in mind that our teaching strategies vary depending on subject, location and age range. It is imperative to know your audience, fundamentally.

Chapter 8

'Your outfit matters' - Mrs A

Believe it or not, what you wear to school matters– more than you think. Not to put any additional pressure on to your already hectic morning of getting ready and out the door on the way to school, but you may need to give some thought to your outfits– they do matter.

At university, we were taught that for everyone, although more specifically targeted at females our outfits should be, 'not too high, not too low, not too slight, not too tight... and so on', this is something that is hugely important as a young teacher who may not have an outfit of teaching clothes established in the early years of teaching.

This saying emphasises the significance of maintaining a professional and appropriate appearance while teaching. As a teacher, your outfit can have a considerable impact on your students' perception of you, their learning environment, and their overall classroom experience.

Teachers are role models for their students, and their outfits can play a significant role in shaping students' behaviour and attitudes. Don't get me wrong, I don't exactly imagine many pupils replicating my specific choice of outfits, they are questionable for an entirely different reason, but the point is by dressing appropriately, teachers can create an atmosphere of respect and professionalism, which can lead to better student engagement and learning outcomes.

Moreover, the saying 'not too high, not too low, not too slight, not too tight' highlights the importance of choosing outfits that are neither overly casual nor overly formal. This balance can help teachers maintain a sense of authority while still appearing approachable and relatable to their students. We don't necessarily need to maintain the same standard of the bygone days where teachers wear their teaching clocks and walk down the school corridor like some sort of sci-fi villain with a breathing problem, but we do need to maintain a level of professionalism that doesn't involve shorts and a football top.

Chapter 9

'Keep your phone out of sight' - Mrs K

It's hard to deny it, but in today's digital age, mobile phones have become an integral part of our lives– even as far as making notes for this very book, I walk about my school, my head buried into my notes app, jotting down everything I see that could be my muse for a chapter or two. However, their presence in the classroom can be a source of distraction for both teachers and students.

As teachers, we must maintain our focus on teaching and ensure that we are fully engaged with their students. A teacher's attention should be on delivering the lesson effectively and addressing any queries or concerns that students may have. However, we all do it, whether we want to admit it or not, when our phone pings or lights up, almost our instinctive reaction is to immediately glance at it. Which is not ideal in a situation where we must maintain focus on giving the best possible lesson, we can to those children involved.

When teachers are constantly checking their phones, it sends a message to students that they are not fully committed to the class. This can lead to a lack of engagement and motivation among students, ultimately affecting their learning experience. At the end of the day, how can we expect children to remain focused and be eager to learn when the teacher teaching it doesn't seem all that bothered on the lesson, and would rather check a notification on their phone about something like their screentime– ironic isn't it?

We as teachers are role models for our students. By keeping their phones out of sight, we demonstrate the importance of discipline, concentration, and respect for the learning environment. Most schools now practise a zero tolerance to mobile phones throughout the day, if we preach to children that they shouldn't have their mobiles out, then we should follow the same mantra. This ultimately sets a good example to the children and allows us to keep our ears to the ground and be the best possible proactive educator we can be.

That being said however, while it is generally advisable for teachers to keep their personal mobile phones out of sight during teaching hours, there may be certain situations where exceptions can be made.

In case of an emergency, teachers may need to have their phones within reach. However, they should ensure that the volume is muted and that they only check their phones when absolutely necessary.

If a teacher has a family member who is unwell or facing an emergency, they may need to stay connected. In these situations, teachers should inform their colleagues or the school administration about the situation and ensure that they do not compromise the quality of their teaching. I personally would suggest a digital smart watch that the teacher can wear and briefly glance at should it provide a silenced buzz on their wrist. This doesn't interrupt the flow of the lesson, and also provide a professional way of being in touch with any important notifications they may need.

First and foremost, it is crucial for teachers to prioritise their students' learning experience by minimising distractions in the classroom. Keeping personal mobile phones out of sight during teaching hours is an essential step towards maintaining focus and setting a positive example for students. However, there may be specific circumstances where exceptions can be made, such as emergency contacts or urgent family matters. Teachers should be mindful of these exceptions, replying to that Snapchat is not an acceptable exception! Teachers need to ensure that they do not compromise the learning environment.

Chapter 10

'Every teacher is a teacher of Maths and English' —
Mr J

When I was at school, one of the subjects I enjoyed most was Maths, I wasn't much good at it, but I enjoyed it nonetheless. Ironically, a subject I was quite good at, but loathed was English– for both however, when I gave them up and went down to a more niche selection of subjects for A level, I wasn't entirely disappointed. You can imagine my horror then when I came to the harrowing conclusion very early on in my first year of teaching that 'every teacher is a teacher of Maths and English.'

This statement underscores the importance of numeracy and literacy skills in all areas of education. While it may seem counterintuitive to suggest that a Physical Education teacher or a Technology and Design teacher is also a teacher of Maths and English, the reality is that these foundational skills are integral to success in any academic discipline. This concept has been widely discussed and supported by educators, researchers, and policymakers with far more experience, understanding and wisdom than I... I just wish someone had told me...

Numeracy, which encompasses mathematical skills and concepts, is essential for understanding and interpreting data, making informed decisions, and solving real-world problems. In the context of various subjects, numeracy plays a crucial role. For example, in Science classes, students need to analyse data, understand measurements, and grasp mathematical relationships to comprehend scientific concepts. Similarly, in History classes, students may need to interpret graphs or analyse statistical information related to historical events or demographic trends.

Likewise, literacy skills, including reading, writing, and communication, are fundamental for learning across all subjects. Whether it's interpreting primary sources in History, comprehending complex texts in English itself, or writing lab reports in Science, literacy skills are indispensable. Furthermore, effective communication is vital in all academic disciplines as students are required to articulate their thoughts and ideas clearly.

It is widely acknowledged that teachers play a crucial role in shaping the academic and intellectual development of students. While subject-specific knowledge is essential for effective teaching, proficiency in foundational subjects such as Mathematics and English is equally important, if not more so.

Regardless of the subject you teach, you need to possess a strong educational background in Maths and English to effectively impart knowledge and skills to their students.

The Maths department in my school will love me for saying this, but Mathematics is a fundamental subject that underpins various disciplines and real-world applications- it is arguable the most used subject in the education system. Teachers who are well-educated in Mathematics can effectively convey mathematical concepts, problem-solving strategies, and critical thinking skills to their students. Moreover, Maths proficiency enables educators to identify and address misconceptions, provide differentiated instruction, and foster a positive attitude towards the subject among students. Whether teaching Mathematics directly or incorporating mathematical concepts into other subjects, teachers with a solid foundation in Maths can enhance the overall quality of education.

It is as simple as knowing how to work out a percentage. Not to sound like a Maths exam paper, but 'if little pupil X gets 34 out of 40 in their test, what is their overall percentage?' is a common question that you must ask yourself every time you mark a test, so knowing how to effectively work out percentage is hugely beneficial to a teacher regardless of the subject in which they teach.

Not to leave the English department out of my praising, having a sound knowledge of the English language is essential for effective communication, comprehension, and expression across all academic domains. Teachers who are well-versed in English can model proper language usage, facilitate meaningful discussions, and guide students in developing strong literacy skills. Additionally, a strong command of English enables educators to create engaging learning materials, provide constructive feedback on written work, and promote critical reading and writing abilities among students. Regardless of the subject matter being taught, the ability to communicate clearly and effectively in English is indispensable for fostering an enriching learning environment.

In either regard, being able to set a good standard of English and Maths as a teacher is imperative, regardless of subject or age group taught.

Chapter 11

'A to-do list is never really done' – Mrs H

The topic of this chapter is hard to believe given that was given to me by one of the most organised teachers I have ever met in my teaching career thus far– however, that does prove the analogy of the duck above and below the water. While upwardly the duck may appear calm and relaxed, if you put your head below the water– you would see that the duck is paddling away, trying to keep afloat in a sea of marking... lesson planning... photocopying... replying to emails... oh, and a full day of teaching.

The harsh truth is that being a teacher is a demanding and rewarding profession, but it comes with an ever-growing to-do list that seems to never be completed. Teachers are constantly contending with additional work being added to their list every time they take something off it. This phenomenon can be likened to the mythological figure Sisyphus, who was condemned to roll a boulder up a hill only to have it roll back down each time he neared the top. Similarly, teachers often find themselves in a cycle of completing tasks only to have new ones added, making it seem like their to-do list is never truly finished.

One of the reasons why a teacher's to-do list is never truly done is the nature of the profession itself. Teaching involves not only delivering lessons but also planning, marking, attending meetings, communicating with parents, and participating in professional development activities. Each of these tasks requires time and effort, and as soon as one task is completed, another one takes its place. For example, a teacher may spend hours marking past papers only to realise that they need to prepare materials for the next day's lesson or attend a meeting after school. Think about it like this, painting the Golden Gate Bridge. It is said that as soon as the painters finish coating the entire bridge, it is time to start over again from the beginning. Similarly, teachers often find themselves in a perpetual cycle of completing tasks only to have new ones added, whether it's adapting to new curriculum standards, attending professional development workshops, or addressing individual student needs.

Another example can be drawn from the world of technology. Just as software developers release updates and patches to fix bugs and add new features, teachers are constantly updating their teaching methods and materials to meet the evolving needs of their students and the educational landscape.

The never-ending nature of a teacher's to-do list can have significant implications for their well-being and work-life balance. The constant influx of tasks can lead to feelings of overwhelm, stress, and burnout. Teachers may find themselves working long hours, sacrificing personal time, and struggling to find moments of respite amidst the demands of their profession.

Moreover, the perpetual nature of the to-do list can also impact job satisfaction and morale. When teachers feel like they can never truly complete their tasks or achieve a sense of closure, it can diminish their sense of accomplishment and fulfilment in their role.

Despite the challenges posed by the ever-growing to-do list, there are strategies that teachers can employ to manage their workload more effectively. Prioritising tasks based on urgency and importance, setting realistic expectations for what can be accomplished in each timeframe, delegating responsibilities when possible, and practicing self-care are all essential strategies for navigating the unending demands of teaching.

A teacher's to-do list is indeed never ever done. The profession demands continuous adaptation and responsiveness to new challenges and responsibilities. By acknowledging this reality and implementing effective strategies for managing workload and well-being, teachers can navigate the perpetual cycle of tasks with resilience and purpose.

Chapter 12

'Manners cost nothing' – Mrs McK

The idea that manners cost nothing, should be obvious– however in today's modern times, it would seem that manners is a missing commodity in society.

As a teacher, the idea that 'manners cost nothing' is a powerful and essential principle to embody and impart to students. Good manners are not only a reflection of respect and consideration for others but also serve as an example of positive behaviour and communication. By consistently demonstrating good manners, teachers set a standard for their students to follow, fostering a positive and respectful learning environment.

One of the most impactful ways for teachers to instil the value of good manners in their students is by setting a good example themselves. When teachers consistently exhibit polite and respectful behaviour, it sends a clear message to students about the importance of manners in interactions with others. This sets the tone for the classroom environment and encourages students to emulate these behaviours.

Having good manners as a teacher can lead to numerous positive outcomes. Firstly, it creates a welcoming and inclusive atmosphere in the classroom, where students feel valued and respected. This, in turn, can enhance student engagement and participation in learning activities. Additionally, good manners contribute to effective communication between the teacher and students, fostering trust and understanding. Moreover, by modelling good manners, teachers can positively influence students' social and emotional development, preparing them for success in their future interactions and endeavours.

Think of manners within teaching, just as oil lubricates the moving parts of a machine. It allows it to function smoothly and efficiently, good manners grease the wheels of social interactions within the classroom. Without this lubrication, friction may arise, hindering the flow of communication and cooperation. Therefore, just as oil is indispensable for the optimal performance of a machine, good manners are essential for creating an environment conducive to learning and growth.

Embodying good manners as a teacher not only sets an exemplary standard for students but also fosters an environment where respect, understanding, and effective communication thrive. By consistently demonstrating and promoting good manners, teachers can positively impact their students' personal development and academic success.

Period 1

Chapter 13

'Your classroom, Your kingdom'- Mr L

When I first arrived in my current school, the room that was assigned to me, was blank, and it remained blank for a long time. Until one day, as I was sitting typing meticulous lesson plans, or on my phone- I can't remember specifically, I thought, 'that wall looks very bland, too bland, why not do this?' and so I did, that began six months of coloured printing and laminating like a mad man and just before the tail end of the school term, my room, was MY room. As a Technology and Design teacher, I had safety signs, third angle perspective drawings and even a 'periodic table of wood'. To everyone else, my room was probably their idea of hell, but to me, my room was my kingdom, a place where I wanted to come into every morning.

Personalising the classroom environment is an essential aspect of effective teaching. It allows teachers to showcase their own personality, engage students, and create a comfortable learning space, not only for the pupils but for the teacher teaching within as well.

One way to make the classroom environment more personal is by incorporating elements of your own personality and interests. This can include displaying personal photographs, mementos, or artwork that reflect your unique style. Every Christmas card, thank you card and drawing a pupil has given me in my time as a teacher, is proudly displayed on my wall in my classroom. To this day, pupils come into my room and ask, 'is that my card I got you sir?' and I proudly respond, 'yeah of course it is!'. These items can help students connect with you on a more personal level and create a sense of familiarity.

It sounds simple and obvious but by personalising the classroom by arranging the furniture and learning materials in a way that best suits your teaching style and the needs of your students, is a great way to put your stamp on the place. Particularly if you are replacing a member of staff who used to teach in that room, older year groups may be less likely to compare you to your predecessor, if they come into your room on the first day and it looks nothing like that of Mr or Mrs 'such and such'. This might involve rearranging desks, creating designated areas for group work or independent study, and organising resources in a way that is easily accessible to students and yourself.

In addition to incorporating your own personality, it is essential to create an environment that is inclusive and respectful of all students. This can be achieved by ensuring that the classroom is free from any offensive or inappropriate materials, and by creating a safe space for open dialogue and discussion. You may be tempted to put a poster up of your favourite football team or band– this will bring more unwanted attention than wanted and distract the pupils from their overall goal from being in that room, learning.

While putting your stamp on your room and personalising the classroom environment is essential, it is equally important to adhere to the school's policies and guidelines. These policies exist to ensure a consistent learning experience for all students, as well as to maintain a professional atmosphere. Many schools have content that is printed and insist on having them in all classrooms, this may be a range of resources from the basics of spelling, punction or grammar, to safeguarding and emergency signs. Rather than offending those who have asked for these items to be placed in every room, it would be best to ensure that they stay in place. However, that doesn't mean they can't get moved to fit in with your format and vision for the room.

As a helpful tip, consider involving students in the personalisation process, allowing them to have input on the design and organisation of the classroom. This can help create a sense of ownership and responsibility among students and ensures that they can feel as part of the experience as possible. This doesn't mean that you allow them carte blanche on your class, at the end of the day, you are the person who has to look at the room the most, but it would be mutually beneficial for you both if you offered house/reward points for collecting some printing, removing pins or laminating, after you have shown them exactly what to do; the closed end goes in first!!

Chapter 14

'Your own opinions'- Mr J

Despite what you may think in the moment, it is imperative to realise that your opinions, are exactly that; yours.

As a teacher in a school, it is essential to maintain a professional demeanour and keep your opinions to yourself. This not only helps create a conducive learning environment but also promotes respect and trust between you, your students and your colleagues.

A teacher's primary role is to impart knowledge and guide students in their academic journey. It is crucial to remember that your opinions, while valuable in some circumstances, are not the sole determinant of what your students should learn. As an educator, you must be open to different perspectives and encourage your students to think critically and independently. Often you may find yourself in a situation where pupils say, 'oh I don't like him' and you perhaps agree, it is important that you do not let them know this, we as professionals need to remain impartial to the outside world.

As a teacher, it is essential to maintain a neutral stance and remain impartial on various topics, especially those that may be politically or emotionally charged. By doing so, you create an inclusive environment where all students feel comfortable expressing their thoughts and opinions without fear of judgment or ridicule. There is simply no place for your opinions, and often there's no place for the pupils' opinions either if they aren't relevant to that of the learning going on. That being said, it is often hard when pupil is slagging off your beloved football team or a teacher you are close with, to not interject with your own opinions

Keeping your opinions to yourself helps foster a safe and supportive learning environment. When students feel that their teacher is approachable and non-judgmental, they are more likely to share their ideas, ask questions, and participate actively in class discussions. This, in turn, leads to a more engaging and effective learning experience for everyone involved.

On top of this, keeping your opinions to yourself, you encourage your students to develop their critical thinking skills. When you allow your students to express their thoughts and opinions, you give them the opportunity to learn how to analyse, evaluate, and synthesise information. This helps them become more independent learners and thinkers, which is essential for their future success. I know from personal experience that from an early point of your career, you don't necessarily think in that way. As a young professional you want to make your mark and that often means sharing your opinions and asking children to conform with them almost, but in reality, you realise that that is counterproductive to your primary objective as an educator. By pushing your opinions, you are conforming children into the same belief system as yours, thus creating sheep rather than competent independent thinkers. By creating sheep within the education system, we create a stagnated mindset that falls behind with the times.

As a teacher, you are a role model for your students. By keeping your opinions to yourself and demonstrating respect and professionalism, you set a positive example for your students to follow.

This helps them understand the importance of treating others with kindness, empathy, and understanding, both in and out of the classroom and is ultimately something that this world is somewhat currently lacking in modern times.

Chapter 15

'Stand your ground'- Mrs McK

Picture the scene, you're a young teacher, you're just fresh in the door of the school from university and the bus duty rota has just been released for the year. You scan down it, and you see that you've hit the jackpot; a handy Wednesday afternoon bus duty at the part of the school where the bus comes and goes within five minutes. Happy days! However, then a more seasoned teacher comes to you and asks can you swap duties with them, usually accompanied with some excuse that makes you feel compelled to oblige. You ask them, 'when is your duty?', they say that it's the last bus out the gates on a Friday afternoon and that it would 'go a long way in this place if you were seen to be a team player'.

Of course, you might think, 'I've nothing to do on Friday afternoons, and even if I don't get noticed to be doing it, it will be helping someone out', and if you think that, by all means oblige with the seasoned teacher. However, if you perhaps have youth club or a recurring arrangement scheduled for that time and you can't do it, do not feel obliged to facilitate the request. This may be a simple case of where the seasoned teacher is trying to impart their experience and position within the school on to you as a 'baby teacher' in an attempt to benefit themselves. If you feel like this may be the case, or that you simply cannot do it for them, say that you can't, and most importantly– stand your ground. They may choose to ask again, perhaps this time in a slightly different tone, or even go above you and tell the principal that you agreed to swap, this does not change anything, if you haven't agreed to swap, stand your ground and say so; do not roll over and accept it because this teacher has gone and spoke to the boss about it. Don't forget, you can do the same.

If you chose to roll over and accept it; it starts a bad precedent for future encounters with this teacher.

Where possible, stand your ground on your opinions and beliefs within the school, not just with trivial things like a bus duty, but with more important things on a professional level. It demonstrates professionalism and confidence in one's abilities as an educator if you can strongly fight for what you believe in, be that departmentally or within a differing belief with a colleague who perhaps teaches the content differently and disagrees with how you do. When faced with disagreements or differing opinions among colleagues, standing your ground allows for constructive dialogue and the exchange of ideas while maintaining mutual respect.

However, this mindset can also be adapted for pupils as well, standing your ground as a teacher helps to establish and maintain authority in the classroom. When students perceive their teacher as confident and assertive, they are more likely to respect the teacher's instructions and guidelines. In university, we were taught two mantras to follow when in the classroom, the first being that we were to 'go in hard and come out soft'; this refers to being assertive, and confident in the classroom from September to the New Year which then allows for an established classroom and what it is going to be like. The second pearl of wisdom we were taught is 'don't smile until Christmas'; this in itself is a lot more difficult, but if you can achieve this, it can lead to better classroom management and improved student behaviour– the pupils may think you are the modern day version of a German dictator but they will respect you and learn a lot better than if you were weak in your assertiveness. Additionally, standing your ground can prevent students from testing boundaries and pushing limits, ultimately creating a more disciplined and focused learning environment.

By standing your ground, teachers can effectively set boundaries with students. This involves communicating clear expectations regarding behaviour, academic performance, and classroom rules. When teachers consistently enforce these boundaries, it fosters a sense of structure and predictability for students. As a result, students understand the consequences of their actions and are more likely to adhere to the established guidelines.

This is a very hard thing to achieve as a young NQT, when you have twenty-five children trying to dictate the odds. However, with that being said, it does click with you eventually; despite how it may seem. I remember one occasion in my first year of teaching where I couldn't maintain classroom control on a class; I went to a few more seasoned teachers on the top floor of the school, as they sat and drank tea stronger than Geoff Capes, one said the words that stuck with me right until the day it eventually did; 'don't worry, one day it will click, it might be tomorrow, it might be next year, it might be five years from now, but it will, and it will get easier from that point onwards'. Eventually, at some point I don't remember specifically when, it did click, and that's the moment when I realised, I can maintain consistency and stand my ground; thus, resulting in better classroom discipline.

While I'm not advocating for you as the reader to become a teacher similar to that of a horse that will not lead nor drive, I do believe that standing your ground as a teacher plays a crucial role in building trust and respect among students and colleagues. When teachers uphold their principles and remain steadfast in their decisions, it conveys integrity and reliability. This can lead to stronger relationships with students based on mutual respect and trust. Similarly, colleagues are more likely to value the input of a teacher who stands their ground on important educational matters. As a teacher it is essential for maintaining authority, setting boundaries, promoting professionalism among colleagues, fostering a positive learning environment, and building trust and respect within the school community.

Chapter 16

'Keep the real people sweet'- Ms B

At university you're taught the hierarchy of school, they teach you that at the top is the principal, then the vice-principal, then the senior teachers, then the heads of departments and years and then finally, at the bottom of the pile, you; a lowly little NQT who has just walked through the door, and while that is typically the proper order of things, and ultimately what keeps the school moving, I learnt on my first day on the job, that there's other people responsible for keeping the school afloat, and these people are the true ones you need to keep sweet.

On my first day of teacher, I was given a tour of the school by the schools teacher tutor. As we walked up and down the long corridors, she filled my head with information that, I'm not sure I even remembered by the end of the day, let alone now; but what stuck in my head was the immortal lines that thus informed this chapter. 'Keep the real people sweet', she told me that if you want anything done in this school there's a few people who will get it done, like that of those prison films you see, the right people will get the right job done. Simply put, the caretaker, the receptionists, the reprographics guy and the head of teacher cover are the ones who if you have them on your side, you're well in there.

On an individual level, the caretaker is the ace card of the deck, responsible for maintaining the cleanliness and safety of the school premises. Building a good rapport with the caretaker can lead to a more pleasant and well-maintained environment for everyone at the school. Additionally, if any issues arise regarding facilities or maintenance, having a positive relationship with the caretaker can facilitate work getting done just that bit quicker, which is always a bonus. This is not to mention that the caretaker is the one person in the school who has access to everywhere, they likely know more about you than you do yourself, so keeping them onside is always a benefit for finding out the comings and goings of the place.

As I've mentioned previously, I was a head of year for a while, in that time I came across many difficult characters who were looking to get a hold of me and tell me that I was doing my job entirely incorrectly. The schools receptionists are the first line of defence for any teacher. They beat away unnecessary phone calls or difficult conversations just far enough for you to compose yourself and ready a plan, this often means they are at the brunt of the disgruntled parents attack, taking the flack and absorbing it like it is nothing. Generally, the receptionists are the first people you see as you walk through the school doors, keeping them on side is always a good way to start the day.

My school's reprographics guy does everything, literally everything. What he doesn't know, you won't need to know. A person responsible for the photocopying, ordering and supplying of resources including projectors, laminating pouches and ink for printers is literally the most powerful person in a school. If a principal is a car dealer, a reprographics person is the fuel supplier, both jobs important, but one can't work without the other whereas one can work without the other. Keeping a reprographics person sweet is always a sure-fire way to have access to the coloured printer or twenty-four-hour IT support where needed. A few years back, we had a paper shortage in the school, literally one reem per department and just like pupils in the school playground, if you had paper, you were the cool guy with the chewing gum everyone wanted to be friends with all of sudden. When the repo guy got a new supply of paper in, the quality was different; better. To this day, we still talk about that supply of paper, and he is treated like a hero for it. When the time came that the new supply came in, my department was one of the first to get the goods. Always good to have a good supplier who you have on your side.

Finally, but certainly no means least is the head of teacher cover. This person is the key, to you not having to teach. Think about that. This person is the one that decides if you can have time off or not. By keeping this person sweet, its beneficial to you. In most schools there is an absence request procedure, in mine, we call it the blue form. This process sees the form going to the principal to be approved and then sent to the teacher in charge of cover, then you get off, a lengthy process. However, if you have a last-minute appointment the next day, there isn't always time for that whole procedure, by keeping the head of cover on side, you may be able to drop a text, 'hey... can I have the 21st off', as simple as that. While this isn't always possible, if the head of cover likes you, they may be more likely to facilitate your request. Not to mention; if you have them on your side or indeed not on your side, that can be the difference between having to tidy your classroom or not upon your return. Depending on who the head of cover puts into your room to cover you, you may have a bombsite to walk into or you may have all the work done, neatly piled on your desk. This person controls who covers you, someone competent is always preferred, but that isn't your choice, it is theirs.

By no means am I saying you should neglect everyone else in the school and stick around these people. Everyone has a unique role to play in the tapestry of a school setting, however, these people play a huge part in whether or not your teaching life is easy or difficult, so better to keep them on your Christmas card list where possible if you can.

Chapter 17

'Recognise everyone equally'- Mrs K

It should go without saying, however unfortunately in today's society, it does need to be said. Everyone is equal. My mum always says, 'it doesn't matter if you're sweeping the streets or the man that runs the country, you're equal' and she has a point. In a school setting, everyone is equal. A well-functioning school depends on everyone knowing their role and sticking to it, but a well-functioning self-respecting school is a school in which the staff within recognise that everyone involved has a unique and equally valued role.

As a young teacher, it is crucial to recognise and appreciate the fact that every individual within the school environment plays an equally important role in the functioning and success of the institution. This includes not only the school principal and teachers but also extends to support assistants, administrative staff, maintenance personnel, and even the classroom cleaners. Each person's contribution is integral to creating a conducive and effective learning environment for students.

Recognising the significance of every role within the school fosters a sense of collaboration and unity among all staff members. When each person's contribution is valued and acknowledged, it creates a positive work culture where everyone feels respected and appreciated. This, in turn, leads to improved morale and job satisfaction across the entire school community.

When every individual within the school feels valued and recognised for their contributions, it directly impacts the student experience. A collaborative and supportive environment among staff members translates into a more positive and nurturing atmosphere for students. It sets an example of respect and inclusivity, which can positively influence students' attitudes towards teamwork and mutual respect.

Recognising the equal importance of every role in the school setting also promotes professional growth among staff members. When individuals feel that their contributions are valued, they are more likely to be motivated to excel in their roles. This can lead to increased productivity, innovation, and a willingness to continuously improve in their respective positions.

By acknowledging the significance of every role within the school, a stronger sense of community is cultivated. When all staff members feel that they are integral parts of the school's success, it creates a shared sense of purpose and belonging. This can lead to stronger relationships among colleagues and a more unified approach towards achieving common goals.

Fundamentally a key lesson to take away from this is as a young teacher, recognising the equal importance of every role within the school setting is fundamental to creating a harmonious and successful educational environment. By fostering collaboration, enhancing the student experience, promoting professional growth, and building a stronger community, acknowledging the value of each individual's contribution ultimately contributes to the overall success of the school. By being able to do this, not only do you foster a sense of community within the school, but you also can be seen as a 'team player' and a part of the school family.

Chapter 18

'Professional at all times, personal no'- Mr R

As a teacher, especially that of a young teacher, it is crucial to always maintain a professional demeanour. This means refraining from allowing personal matters to interfere with your interactions with students, colleagues, and parents. By upholding professionalism, educators can create a positive and effective learning environment. There is no hard and fast rule for this however, as educations we walk a fine line- this chapter doesn't remove said line, but it does hopefully enlighten a way in which we can widen the line we walk daily.

University will teach you, that professionalism is universal, and to an extent it is, however, one thing I have learnt, is depending on several different factors, the definition of professional changes. It can change with the location of the school, the year group and even the subject you teach.

In the classroom, it is essential for teachers to set a professional tone. This involves using appropriate language. This is one aspect of remaining professional that I initially struggled with in my first year of teaching. My school was based in the centre of the country, literally the schools' neighbours were sheep and woodland animals, however up until that point, I had only ever taught on teaching practise, which was always based in larger towns or cities. While there is nothing wrong with either location, the language you use to children based in a more urban area is certainly different to that of the language you use in a country setting. Up until that point, I thought 'well' was a large hole with water in it, whereas on my first day of teaching, I realised that it is a greeting in that part of the world. Very quickly you can lose the attention of the children you are tasked to teach if you don't approach them in a manner they can relate to.

Another crucial aspect that will vary depending on location, education level or subject, is the dress code- while professionalism is always needed with our outfits, there are many definite distinguishing factors on how we dress. Tie, no tie, brown boots, no brown boots, waist coat, no waist coat for example are all considerations based upon where, who and what you are teaching.

Not only with pupils, maintaining professionalism extends to interactions with colleagues. Teachers should avoid gossiping or engaging in unprofessional behaviour with their peers. For instance, if a teacher disagrees with a colleague's approach to a certain issue, it is important to address the matter privately and respectfully rather than engaging in public confrontations or spreading around in the staffroom. Equally so, while it is often difficult, if we are ever faced with an instance where someone is speaking about another person in a negative way, it is important that unless we directly are involved, we don't involve ourselves. This in turn will disassociate yourself with the situation and ultimately mean you don't receive any unwarranted attention.

One of the most difficult ways to remain professional that I have found is when communicating with parents, in the early days of my tenure as Head of Year I vividly remember emailing my teacher tutor, asking how to approach parents so that I don't get a call back to complain, or worse, my line manager does. It is crucial for teachers to maintain professionalism. This means refraining from discussing personal matters or grievances with parents and focusing on the academic and behavioural progress of the students. Often you may find that a parent has an explanation as to why their child is not performing as well academically anymore or perhaps performing too well as the school's resident pain in the neck. Whatever excuse they provide, while you can disagree and challenge if you have the evidence to back it up, if you feel personally, it is wrong and have no evidence of such, do not express that personal opinion. Another trap parents often lay is they often provide another pupils name as the excuse as to why their son or daughter is not as should be- under no circumstances should teachers engage in a session of berating the other pupil. Stay away from lines such as 'yeah, I agree, little Jimmy is....' Because what you may find is that parent, knows the parent of little Jimmy and will easily go to them and say, 'Mr or Mrs such and such says that...'. Which then leaves you as an educator wide open for the backlash of both the initial parent and little Jimmy's as well.

Failing to uphold professionalism can have detrimental effects on both the teacher and the learning environment. It can lead to strained relationships with students, colleagues, and parents, ultimately impacting the effectiveness of teaching and learning. Additionally, unprofessional behaviour can tarnish a teacher's reputation and credibility within the school community. Often, we forget that the teaching profession is actually quite small. Everyone has a contact of a contact in another school, it takes the three levels of separation theory to an entire new level. What this means is that if we are seen to be unprofessional and then we approach another school via application or word of mouth. You can near enough guarantee that someone in that school has heard of you or knows someone who works with you and can easily find out about you. 'Your name travels further than you do' comes to mind.

Chapter 19

'You don't always have to say yes'- Miss O

As a young teacher, it is essential to understand the importance of setting boundaries and learning to say no when necessary. While it is natural to want to be accommodating and helpful to colleagues, students, and parents, especially in the pursuit of a permanent job, it is equally important to recognise when saying yes, may compromise your well-being or professional responsibilities. There is no shame in learning to assert oneself and set boundaries early in one's teaching career, that ultimately can lead to a more sustainable and fulfilling experience in the long run, where you often may find that people don't put you in the situation of having to say yes as often.

Don't get me wrong, some people are programmed to be 'people pleasers'. I myself am one. Someone who would bend over backwards for anyone and ask nothing in return. Its something that I have done for years, and I am not alone. Those who are like this can be broken down into two categories of 'people pleaser'. Intrinsic and extrinsic.

Intrinsic and extrinsic motivation are two different types of motivation that drive individuals to behave in certain ways. Intrinsic motivation refers to engaging in an activity for its own sake because it is inherently satisfying, while extrinsic motivation involves engaging in an activity to earn a reward or avoid punishment. People who are intrinsically motivated are driven by internal factors such as personal enjoyment, interest, or a sense of accomplishment, whereas those who are extrinsically motivated are driven by external factors such as money, praise, or recognition. Regardless of which one you may be, if you are either, you are, a 'people pleaser'. You're not a leper however if you are someone who wants the best for someone else rather than yourself, regardless of the motivation behind it. You just need to be aware that in a school setting, it may be something which others may lean on and use to their advantage.

In a previous chapter, I gave an example of being asked by a colleague to swap bus duty from a Wednesday to a Friday. Despite feeling hesitant about saying no, it is imperative that if you do not want to do it, you are not obliged to do so. By respectfully declining the request and explaining the reasons, you demonstrate the importance of setting boundaries and prioritising a balance between professional commitments and social needs.

Learning to say no as a young teacher does not mean being uncooperative or unsupportive. It means understanding one's limitations and being able to communicate effectively with colleagues, students, and parents about what is feasible and reasonable within the scope of one's responsibilities. Just because you are the new guy does not mean you are contracted to say 'yes' to everyone.

By setting boundaries and learning when to say no, young teachers can establish healthy work-life balance and maintain their well-being while fulfilling their roles effectively.

While some individuals may be naturally inclined towards intrinsic motivation, it is crucial for young teachers to recognise the significance of setting boundaries and learning when to say no.

By understanding the distinction between intrinsic and extrinsic motivation and applying this knowledge in professional interactions, young teachers can navigate their roles with confidence and integrity, and ultimately avoid getting taken advantage of.

Chapter 20

'Every day is different'- Mrs S

It sounds stupid, but the term 'every day is a school day' is highly accurate in a school setting believe it or not, however another saying that is appropriate and applicable to a school setting is 'every day is different'.

It encapsulates the dynamic nature of the educational environment, where each day presents new challenges, opportunities, and experiences for both students and educators.

As a teacher, one encounters a multitude of variables that contribute to this dynamism. For instance, the composition of students in a class varies from day to day due to factors such as absences, new enrolments, or changes in group dynamics. This constant flux necessitates adaptability on the part of the teacher, as they must tailor their approach to accommodate these fluctuations. At university we are taught to plan our lessons, almost to a perfect degree of accuracy under 'perfect' conditions where there isn't any absenteeism, ongoing pastoral issues or group dynamics. This concept works in principal while on teaching practise where you are wrapped in bubble wrap and given the best behaved class in the year, but in an ideal world, as a result of a school being an every changing tapestry, there really is a lot of variables to plan for, and it is near impossible to predict what is going to come on the day you plan for, until that very day.

Moreover, the content being taught also contributes to the ever-changing nature of each day. Whether it's introducing new material, revisiting previous concepts, or addressing student inquiries, the subject matter itself adds layers of diversity to each day in the classroom. This necessitates flexibility and responsiveness from educators as they strive to meet the evolving needs of their students. This also is applicable to your teaching in general. You may very well have a qualification in Maths, English or even Primary education, however often you may be asked to take on a class that isn't in your wheelhouse, this change means as a teacher we face new challenges in a subject that isn't our speciality. In my first few years of teaching, I was given the subjects of Maths and Science in and above that of my standard Technology and Design specialism, this variation in change, allowed for every period of the subjects I wasn't familiar with to be a bespoke experience.

On any given day, teachers may encounter varying levels of student participation, motivation, and attentiveness. For instance, one day may involve lively discussions and enthusiastic involvement from students, while the next could present challenges related to disengagement or behavioural issues. As a result, teachers must continuously adapt their strategies to foster an inclusive and productive learning environment. Believe it or not, this can even depend on the actual day, or the time of the day in question. I always found a class that I see period one and two on a Monday is a lot more lethargic than the same class I had on a Friday last two. As a result, it would be naive to think every day would be a rinse and repeat experience with every class all the time.

Furthermore, unexpected events or circumstances can significantly impact the daily dynamics within a school. These may range from impromptu assemblies and guest speakers to technical malfunctions or weather-related disruptions. Some may be predictable, some may not be, in either event each leads to an entirely unique day. Within my first year of teaching, I had five snow days, three impromptu bank holidays and a global pandemic! Each brought an entirely unique set of circumstances that as a teacher I had to respond to.

Teachers are compelled to employ diverse instructional approaches tailored to meet the unique demands of each day. This may involve modifying lesson plans on short notice, integrating alternative teaching methods to address student needs effectively, or leveraging technology in response to unforeseen challenges. By embracing adaptability and innovation, educators can navigate through the ever-changing landscape of daily experiences within a school environment.

The multifaceted nature of the classroom environment, coupled with diverse student dynamics and unforeseen events, underscores the truth behind the idea that every day is different. We as educators need to be aware of this and ensure that we are as adaptable as possible. Initially starting out it may be difficult for us to achieve this, having just graduated from university where we have been programmed to think under ideal circumstances- as a result of this can be very daunting for a NQT, however realising this early on can benefit us in the long run going forward. Generally speaking, the mindset of 'what will be will be' works well in this scenario.

Chapter 21

'Things in a school you'll never understand'- Mr O'C

You would be naive to think that as a new teacher to a school you will walk in and know everything about it, but you would be even more so if you thought that after a period of time, you would know most things to do with the school.

The right way of it, however, is that you could work in a school for fifty years and not know everything, it all depends on a need-to-know basis, and since you're the new person in the door- you really don't need to know.

Don't get me wrong, as you climb up the rungs of the ladder to department head, year head, senior teacher, you do unlock new insights and understandings- like a video game character who can only go on a quest when they have gained enough XP.

As educators it is essential to acknowledge that no matter how long you work in a school setting, there will always be gaps in your knowledge. This realisation is crucial as it allows educators to focus on what they do know and leverage the expertise of others to fill in the gaps. Working collaboratively with colleagues who may possess different knowledge and skills can lead to a more effective and efficient school environment.

One of the key aspects of accepting limitations in a school setting is embracing humility. Recognising that no individual can know everything about education fosters a culture of continuous learning and improvement. By acknowledging what one does not know, educators can remain open to new ideas, perspectives, and approaches that can benefit both themselves and their students.

Collaboration among educators is a powerful tool for addressing gaps in knowledge and expertise. By working together, teachers can share insights, strategies, and resources that enhance their collective effectiveness. Collaborative efforts also promote a sense of community within the school environment, fostering a supportive culture where individuals feel valued for their unique contributions.

Accepting the limitations of one's knowledge in a school setting is a fundamental aspect of professional growth and development. By focusing on what one does know and collaborating with others who possess complementary skills, educators can create a more dynamic and effective learning environment for their students.

Chapter 22

'Politics' – Mr M

My granny, God love her, would describe politics in a school in the same way she would describe people's opinions and when you should share them. 'It's like armpits, everyone has them, we don't need to see them because sometimes they stink'- now, I might be slightly biased, but I think in the entirety of this book, that may be the most appropriate, and level-headed quote in here... Sorry Einstein.

When it comes to politics in schools, there is a fine line between what belongs and what does not belong.

Often there is a place for politics in a school as it allows students to be exposed to different political ideas and beliefs as part of their education in becoming informed citizens. However, when politics start to interfere with the professional environment of a school, it can become problematic.

When politics start to interfere with the professional environment of a school, it can become problematic. Religion, political beliefs, and even sports affiliations such as football teams are areas where politics may not belong in a school setting. These topics can be divisive and may lead to conflicts among students, teachers, and parents. In a school environment that should prioritise education and inclusivity, introducing these sensitive political topics can create unnecessary tension.

While overt displays of political beliefs may not be appropriate in a school setting, it is important to acknowledge that there is often an undercurrent of backstage politics at play. This can manifest in various ways, such as preferential treatment given to certain students or teachers based on personal relationships or other non-meritocratic factors.

Parker J. Palmer once said, 'The politics of the school are never far from the surface.' This quote highlights the reality that politics, whether visible or hidden, play a role in shaping the dynamics within a school community.

While it is crucial for students to engage with political ideas and concepts as part of their learning experience, it is equally important to maintain a professional and inclusive environment within schools. Balancing these aspects ensures that politics enrich rather than disrupt the educational journey of students.

Period 2

Chapter 23

'Know your audience'- Mr P

A car salesman needs to know about the cars in which he or she sells. He needs to know if that 4x4 is able to tow 6 ton unbraked or if that hatchback has isofix child restraints. If the salesman didn't know anything about the car, I would easily bet no one would buy off them. Similarly, so, as a teacher, understanding your audience is crucial for effective communication and successful learning outcomes. This understanding encompasses various aspects, including pastoral, academic, and individual characteristics of the students. By knowing your audience on these levels, you can tailor your teaching methods to better engage and support them in their learning journey, and ultimately make your life as a teacher all the bit easier.

Probably paramount is knowing your audience pastorally. This involves understanding the personal and emotional aspects of your students. This includes being aware of their backgrounds, cultures, and any challenges they may be facing outside of the classroom, and by knowing our pupils, we can recognise the red flags they are exhibiting. If a pupil happens to be exhibiting tendencies not characteristic of them, my suggestion is taking that extra second that eats into your lunch time to hold that one pupil behind who doesn't seem be themselves. You would be surprised how much gets revealed when no other pupils are in the room, and it's just you and them, and of course, the third person for safeguarding. By recognising these factors and signs, teachers can create a supportive and inclusive environment that nurtures the holistic development of their students. Additionally, having a pastoral understanding allows teachers to provide appropriate support to students who may be dealing with personal issues that could impact their academic performance. Such issues may even need to be brought up to a higher level in the school. As classroom teachers, we are the first line of defence for pastoral issues and identifying them early can mean a situation doesn't develop past the point of rectification.

Going back to the car salesman analogy. If they are selling you a car, and they are talking about the torque in each one of its gears within its sequential semi-automatic gearbox, and you're more focused on if it has enough cup holders, chances are you are going to tune out and lose focus. In the same token understanding your audience academically involves recognising the diverse learning needs and abilities within the classroom. This includes being aware of each student's strengths, weaknesses, and preferred learning styles. If you are pitching at a higher level than they can understand, it will undoubtedly result in a lack of interest, work ethic and an increase in poor behaviour. By acknowledging these differences, teachers can adapt their teaching strategies to cater to the various academic requirements of their students. This may involve differentiating instruction, providing additional support where needed, or offering enrichment opportunities for those who excel in certain areas.

In addition to pastoral and academic considerations, knowing your audience also involves understanding the individual quirks and preferences of each student. This could include recognising how students respond to different communication styles – some may thrive when given clear instructions in a firm manner, while others may require a gentler approach. Understanding these nuances allows teachers to build stronger connections with their students and create an environment where everyone feels valued and understood.

In considering the importance of knowing one's audience as a teacher, it is essential to reflect on the impact of teacher-student dynamics in the classroom environment. The quote 'children suffer more from bores than from brutes' by H.C. Dent encapsulates this idea succinctly. It emphasises that uninspiring or disengaged teaching can have a more detrimental effect on students than strict discipline or harsh behaviour. This quote serves as a reminder of the responsibility teachers have in actively engaging with their students and adapting their approach to meet the diverse needs within the classroom.

Fundamentally, knowing your audience as a teacher is paramount for creating an inclusive and effective learning environment. By understanding students pastorally, academically, and individually, teachers can tailor their approach to better engage and support their students' diverse needs.

Chapter 24

'You don't have to shout'- Mrs M

When writing this book, I canvased every reachable teacher I could. During that canvasing, I received lots of helpful pearls of wisdom that I hope, 24 chapters in, are helping you along your teaching journey.

One such pearl of wisdom came in the form of the words 'you don't have to shout', and while that is a very useful piece of advice, which we will now delve into. I'd like to add that it came from easily one of the strictest teacher in the school, such teacher, that in my first year of teaching I was petrified of all because of my first encounter with her. She was chewing a pupil apart in the corridor as I was walking down it. I remember thinking, 'wow, remind me not to annoy her'

I personally believe that the notion of 'you don't have to shout' can be considered subjective, as it depends on various factors and perspectives.

When exploring both arguments for and against shouting as a form of discipline, it is important to consider the context in which shouting occurs, such as in a loud workshop environment or across a rugby pitch. While it may be acceptable to raise one's voice to be heard over the noise, using shouting as an intimidation tactic may not be conducive to effective discipline. There are alternative methods of disciplining children that do not involve shouting, and these should be considered as well.

In a loud workshop environment or any setting with high levels of ambient noise, raising one's voice may be necessary for effective communication, particularly in the event of where someone may be at risk of injury. In such cases, shouting can be justified as a means of ensuring that instructions or commands are heard and understood by the students, and safety is upheld.

Additionally, some proponents argue that in certain situations, particularly with older students who may be more resistant to authority, raising one's voice can convey a sense of urgency and seriousness that is necessary for maintaining order and discipline. In this case, it may be justified provided the results are effective and it is necessary.

On the other side of the coin, shouting as a form of discipline can have negative psychological effects on students. It can create an atmosphere of fear and intimidation rather than respect and understanding.

Research has shown that excessive shouting or yelling can lead to increased stress levels in children and may hinder their ability to learn effectively. Moreover, there are alternative disciplinary methods such as positive reinforcement, redirection, and setting clear expectations that do not rely on raising one's voice.

The appropriateness of shouting as a form of discipline also depends on the age, subject, and experience of the teacher. Younger teachers or those new to the profession may not have developed alternative disciplinary strategies and may resort to shouting out of frustration or lack of experience. Additionally, different subjects may require different approaches to discipline; for instance, a physical education teacher in a noisy rugby pitch may need to raise their voice to maintain control. Furthermore, school policies and guidelines play a crucial role in shaping teachers' behaviour. If a school encourages non-shouting disciplinary methods and provides training in alternative strategies, teachers may feel more supported in using these methods. It is best to check with the school regarding their policies concerning shouting.

The individual comfort level of the teacher with shouting also plays a significant role. Some educators may feel uncomfortable or morally opposed to raising their voices as a means of discipline, which in any instance is fine. Ultimately the teacher, like all jobs needs to be comfortable with their workplace and what they are being asked to do within it.

Personal beliefs about effective teaching methods and the impact of shouting on students' emotional well-being can influence whether a teacher chooses to employ this approach. Each teacher can take a different stance on the effectiveness shouting and ultimately who is to know who is right and wrong- we as professionals need to remain as such and trust that the correct teaching is being given, regardless of the platter in which it is dished up on.

As a whole approach, there are valid arguments both for and against shouting as a form of discipline in a school setting. It is important for educators to consider the environment around them before making a decision on whether to shout. Factors such as noise levels, student age and behaviour, personal comfort with shouting, and school policies should all be taken into account when determining the appropriateness of using shouting as a disciplinary method.

Ultimately, it will remain a subject of contention for a long time yet.

Chapter 25

'Change Your Tone'- Mr S

As a teacher, the tone you use in the classroom plays a crucial role in creating a positive and effective learning environment. We as effective educators must understand when it is more important and beneficial to use a change of tone as opposed to shouting unnecessarily.

One of the primary reasons for changing your tone as a teacher is to create a positive learning environment. The way you communicate with your students greatly influences their engagement and motivation. By using a calm and respectful tone, you can foster an atmosphere where students feel comfortable expressing themselves and participating actively in class discussions. This positive environment contributes to improved student performance and overall well-being. First and foremost, if we provide a nurturing learning environment for our pupils, it in turn nurtures quality learning and yields results.

The tone used by a teacher has a direct impact on student behaviour. When teachers communicate in a respectful and encouraging manner, students are more likely to respond positively.

On the other hand, shouting or using an aggressive tone can lead to feelings of fear, anxiety, and disengagement among students. Research has shown that positive reinforcement and constructive feedback are far more effective in shaping student behaviour than punitive measures such as shouting or berating. Effective teachers can however change their tone which ultimately achieves a different outcome in the lesson, for example, if a large group of pupils are talking about something irrelevant to that of being taught, a slight tone change to a sterner tone will engage their attention again and you can recant back to your original tone once order has been achieved.

Changing your tone as a teacher is instrumental in building trust and rapport with your students. When students feel that their teacher respects and values them, they are more likely to trust the guidance provided. This trust forms the foundation for meaningful teacher-student relationships, which are essential for academic success and personal development.

As Maya Angelou once said, 'I've learned that people will forget what you said, people will forget what you did, but people will never forget how you made them feel.'

Effective communication is at the heart of successful teaching. By adjusting your tone based on the situation, you can enhance communication with your students. Whether it's delivering instructions, providing feedback, or addressing concerns, a thoughtful and adaptable tone enables clearer and more impactful communication. This fosters an environment where students feel heard and understood, leading to improved learning outcomes.

Changing your tone as a teacher is crucial for creating a positive learning environment, influencing student behaviour positively, building trust and rapport with students, enhancing communication, and promoting emotional well-being. It is far more beneficial than resorting to shouting as it fosters respect, understanding, and empathy while contributing to an environment conducive to learning and growth.

As teachers we can change our tone just slightly and it can change the dynamic of the entire classroom environment. This however is something that is certainly learned through experience as your career goes on.

Chapter 26

'Parents & Pupils Vs You'- Mrs McS

In the realm of modern-day teaching, the dynamics between parents, pupils, and teachers have undergone significant changes. In years gone by, the traditional teacher-student relationship was characterised by a more authoritative approach, where the teacher held the power and was responsible for imparting knowledge to the students. Parents often played a supportive role, working in collaboration with the teacher to ensure the students' academic success. However, this dynamic often resulted in a 'parents and the teacher against the pupils' mentality, particularly when it came to underperformance in school. Often, it made teaching easier for the old guard of teachers to enforce actions, sanctions and consequences when they knew they would be reinforced by their tag team partner, that of the parent.

The advent of modern-day teaching has brought about a paradigm shift in the way education is perceived and delivered. This has led to a more inclusive and collaborative approach, where parents, teachers, and pupils work together to achieve academic success. This new dynamic has also changed the way blame is attributed when it comes to underperformance.

Parents today are more involved in their children's education than ever before. They are often seen as partners in the learning process, working closely with teachers to understand their children's progress and needs. This increased involvement has led to a greater sense of responsibility and accountability on the part of parents, as they are now seen as active contributors to their children's academic success or failure, which on paper sounds ideal, comparing to that of years gone by. My father always says that his father, my grandfather, 'never knew anying about his school life, unless he had done something wrong- then he knew all about it'

In modern day teaching, pupils are no longer passive recipients of knowledge but active participants in their own learning. They are encouraged to take ownership of their education and develop critical thinking and problem-solving skills. This shift in focus has led to a greater emphasis on the responsibility of pupils in their academic performance, however, that greater emphasis is now having its effect on teachers.

Teachers today are expected to be facilitators of learning, guiding and supporting pupils in their educational journey. They are responsible for creating an inclusive and engaging learning environment that caters to the diverse needs of their students. This has led to a shift in the blame culture, where teachers are now often held accountable for underperformance, rather than the pupils.

The National Education Association sums it up best when they said, 'Teachers today are expected to be facilitators of learning, guiding and supporting students in their educational journey, and are almost as accountable for it as if it were their own'.

The dynamics between parents, pupils, and teachers in modern day teaching have evolved significantly. The shift from a more authoritative approach to a collaborative and inclusive one has led to a change in the way blame is attributed for underperformance in school. Today, it is a case of where the pupils are underperforming, and the blame is put on the teacher rather than the pupil. This new paradigm highlights the shared responsibility among all stakeholders in the education system to ensure the success of each student, however, with that it often may seem that the teachers are the 'independent entity' in this new union between the stakeholders.

Teachers are now expected to be a part of this new equal paradigm between themselves, pupils and parents, but are often the scapegoat should a pupil underperform academically.

We as educators need to be accountable to the best of our ability so that our actions can be justified in the event of a mutiny in the union and parents and pupils turn on the teacher. a dramatic turn of the tables since the days of parents and teachers versus the pupil.

Chapter 27

'Keep them on a rope'- Mr B

When I was at school, we had a maths teacher–let's call him Mr B. He was a fantastically gifted 2nd generation teacher who had the best of abilities to keep a class on a rope, a rope of which he could let go of or pull it back at any moment. He was the king of classroom control, and he knew it, and so did we! He had us tightly wrapped around that rope and kept the machine running well, but every so often he would let go of the rope and as a result let go of the control... just a tad. He would crack a joke or share an anecdote that let us know he was human and not the robot we thought he was, he would even smile from time to time! However, just as quick as he let go would he pull the rope back and ultimately pull control back of the class.

Maintaining classroom control is a fundamental aspect of effective teaching and Mr B had that mastered. Every university and teaching book will tell you; it is essential for creating a conducive learning environment and ensuring that students are able to focus on their studies. However, what many teachers don't realise, and what

Mr B did was, that it is equally important for teachers to strike a balance between maintaining control and being relatable and human to the students.

Ergo, this delicate balance can be likened to the rope, where the teacher has the ability to tighten or slacken the control they exert over their students.

In the context of the analogy, the tightly wrapped rope represents the teacher's firm control over the classroom. This control is necessary for establishing discipline, managing behaviour, and facilitating effective learning. When the rope is taut, it signifies that the teacher is in command, setting clear expectations, and ensuring that students adhere to rules and guidelines. This level of control is crucial for creating a structured and organised learning environment where students feel safe and supported and ultimately learn to their best ability. Effective classroom management involves establishing routines, implementing consistent consequences for misbehaviour, and using proactive strategies to prevent disruptions. By maintaining a tight grip on the metaphorical rope, teachers can effectively guide their students through lessons, activities, and transitions, thereby maximising instructional time and minimising distractions. Mr B was able to maintain a tightly wrapped rope for as long as he wanted it to be so, we as a class respected that, and even to an extent feared it as well.

However just as a real rope can be slackened, there are times when it is important for teachers to ease up on their control and allow for more flexibility in the classroom. This can involve fostering open communication, showing empathy towards students' individual needs, and creating opportunities for student autonomy and self-expression. When the rope is slackened, barriers come down, and students may feel more comfortable expressing themselves and engaging in collaborative learning experiences. By loosening their grip on the metaphorical rope, teachers can create a more inclusive and supportive classroom environment. This can lead to increased student motivation, enhanced creativity, and stronger relationships between teachers and students. Allowing for moments of informality and spontaneity can also contribute to a positive classroom culture where students feel valued and respected. For Mr B, this usually came in the form of a witty joke at the expense of someone in the class. God forbid you were the person asked to answer a question in class and you got it wrong, Mr B would by no means demean you, but he would find something to comment on about you... 'did you not look over this last night? Too busy doing your hair?' for example. This for a split second would lower the tone of the class, the barriers would come down and we would all have a giggle.

The most admirable part about Mr B, however, was his ability to regain the control. With one single piercing look from his deeply sunken brown eyes, we all knew, it was time to shut up and keep working. While it is important for teachers to let go of control at times, it is equally crucial for them to know when to pull the rope taut again. This signifies regaining control when necessary to redirect behaviour, refocus attention, or address disruptions. By pulling the rope, teachers assert their authority in a respectful manner, reinforcing boundaries, and reminding students of expectations.

Regaining control does not necessarily mean reverting to strict authoritarianism; rather, it involves re-establishing a sense of order and purpose in the classroom. Teachers can use proactive strategies such as positive behaviour reinforcement, redirection techniques, and restorative practices to address challenges while maintaining a supportive learning environment.

Generally speaking, while I haven't mastered the Mr B look just yet, I pride myself on my ability to play with the rope. I believe maintaining classroom control while also allowing for moments of flexibility is essential for effective teaching. The analogy of the rope illustrates how teachers can navigate between firmness and empathy in their interactions with students. By understanding when to tighten or slacken the metaphorical rope, educators can create an environment that promotes both discipline and understanding, ultimately fostering a positive and productive learning experience for all.

Chapter 28

'Know your stuff, pupils see through you'- Mr D

Contrary to popular belief, children are not stupid. In every classroom, the children know exactly what is going on. In the realm of education, teachers are often faced with the challenge of maintaining credibility and authority while simultaneously ensuring that they are providing accurate and up-to-date information to their students and if this can't be done, the children will see through you entirely.

To effectively educate students, teachers must possess a deep understanding of the subject matter they are teaching. This includes not only the core concepts but also the context in which they exist. For instance, a History teacher should not only know the dates and events of historical occurrences but also the cultural, social, and political factors that influenced them. This comprehensive understanding allows teachers to provide a more holistic and engaging learning experience for their students. One thing I learnt very early on in my first year out, was there will always be one child that asks that one question outside of what has been taught- having a sound subject knowledge will greatly go in your favour to provide creditability to not only the pupil but also the class in general.

Aside from subject-specific knowledge, teachers must also be familiar with school rules and policies. This familiarity ensures that they can effectively guide students through the educational system while maintaining a safe and orderly learning environment. Teachers who are well-versed in school rules can also help students understand the rationale behind these rules, fostering a sense of responsibility and respect for the institution. Pupils can tell when a teacher is unsure of the school rules and policies, it is why generally speaking, day to day substitutes have more discipline issues than full time members of staff as a result of the unfamiliarity of the school rules they have, of which the pupils challenge. Having a sound understanding of the rules means we as educators can reinforce the rules where necessary when challenged by a difficult pupil.

Furthermore, a helpful awareness of current culture is crucial for teachers to connect with their students and make learning relevant and relatable. Understanding popular trends, social issues, and technological advancements allows teachers to incorporate these elements into their lessons, making them more engaging and accessible for students. In modern times, if teachers can relate their teachings to the new phone released or whatever the latest trend setter is doing often you find there is more engagement with students.

That being said, while it is hugely important to know exactly what you're talking about as an educator, it is also important to understand that teachers hold a position of trust and authority.

Students look up to their teachers as knowledgeable figures who can guide them through their academic journey. When a teacher displays a lack of knowledge or certainty in a particular subject, it can undermine their credibility and negatively impact the students' perception of their teacher. There is absolutely no point in pretending like you know something if you don't. The children are 4-foot lie detectors who will see if you're unsure or just flat out lying.

Being honest with students about one's limitations is essential for maintaining trust and respect. By admitting when they do not know the answer, teachers demonstrate humility and authenticity, which can have a positive impact on the student-teacher relationship. This honesty also encourages students to develop a growth mindset, as they learn that it is acceptable to not know everything and that seeking answers is a vital part of the learning process.

Teachers should not hesitate to tell students that they do not know the answer at the moment. This honesty helps maintain trust and encourages students to ask questions and seek knowledge. A quick line that will solve any instance of this is, 'You know what? I don't know that. But I will get back to you on it'. By committing to finding the answer and sharing it with the class, teachers demonstrate their dedication to continuous learning and their willingness to grow alongside their students.

Another handy way to get yourself out of a situation where you don't know something and don't want to admit that you don't. You can engage the class in a discussion or brainstorming session to see if any students have the answer or can contribute to the topic. This approach fosters collaboration and peer learning, which are valuable skills in today's interconnected world, but almost most importantly, it can also allow you as the teacher slip under the radar on question, avoiding the risk of losing credibility.

There isn't one teacher on this planet that knows everything about their subject, but equally so, there isn't one teacher on this planet that hasn't bluffed, or at least tried to. From experience, I can say that honesty and admitting one's limitations are crucial for maintaining trust and respect in the classroom. When faced with uncertainty, teachers should be transparent about their lack of knowledge, commit to finding the answer, and involve students in the learning process. By adopting these practices, educators can create a more authentic and engaging learning environment that fosters growth, curiosity, and a love for learning in their students.

Chapter 29

'There are kids you will never forget'- Mrs B

If you start working as a secondary school teacher at twenty-one years old, assuming you have ten classes a year, with thirty pupils in each, and teach for say thirty-five years, you at an estimate will teach approximately ten thousand five hundred kids- you will be doing good, if by the end of your teaching career you remember all those children's names. Chances are, you will forget the large majority of them, but there will be the select few that you will never forget.

As a teacher, there are certain students who leave an indelible mark on your memory over the course of your career. These students stand out for various reasons, and their impact on you as an educator can be profound. Over a career, it is inevitable that some pupils will remain in your mind and heart for specific reasons, shaping your teaching practice and leaving a lasting impression.

Throughout your career, there will be students who stand out due to their exceptional academic achievements, their unique talents, or their remarkable personal growth. These students may have demonstrated extraordinary dedication to their studies, excelled in your subject, or overcome significant challenges to succeed academically. Their accomplishments and perseverance serve as a source of inspiration and motivation for you as a teacher. Even this early into my career, I can honestly say there are pupils in which I already know will stay with me in my mind as a result of their personal backstories and experiences they have overcame to thrive.

During 35 odd years of teaching, there will be students with whom you develop strong personal connections. These connections may stem from shared experiences, mutual respect, or the ability to empathise with each other's struggles. These students leave a lasting impact not only because of their academic performance but also because of the meaningful relationships you have built with them.

Again, I can say I hold a close affinity with my first form class I ever had. Their first day in the school was my first day in the school and I have always seen their growth into young adolescents as something that I have been able to personally be involved within since day one. Despite the fact they have multiple form teachers since me, they will always be MY form class.

Certain students leave an enduring mark on your memory by teaching you valuable life lessons. Their unique perspectives, resilience in the face of adversity, or unwavering determination can profoundly impact your own outlook on life and education. These students become not only learners but also teachers, imparting wisdom that stays with you throughout your career.

As you reflect on your career as an educator, these unforgettable students become part of your professional legacy. Their stories and achievements contribute to the narrative of your teaching journey, reminding you of the meaningful impact you have had on countless young lives. They serve as a testament to the lasting influence of dedicated teachers.

Over the span of a teaching career, certain students will undoubtedly remain etched in your memory for specific reasons, be it good or bad. Whether due to their exceptional achievements, personal connections, growth through challenges, or the valuable lessons they imparted to you, these students play a significant role in shaping your identity as an educator and leaving a lasting impact on your professional journey.

Chapter 30

'Respect goes both ways'- Mrs McK

Mutual respect between teachers and pupils is a fundamental aspect of a healthy and productive learning environment. It is essential for both parties to recognise and appreciate each other's perspectives, abilities, and contributions.

Fundamentally, as children we are taught that respect is a two-way street. This goes for the teacher-pupil relationship. Both parties must acknowledge each other's value and treat one another with consideration and dignity. Just as the teacher expects respect from their students, they must also demonstrate respect towards their students. This reciprocal dynamic fosters a positive and supportive learning environment.

Think of it like a bridge. Just as a bridge requires support from both ends to remain stable and functional, the teacher-pupil relationship relies on mutual respect to thrive. Without this mutual support, the bridge becomes unstable, hindering the flow of knowledge and understanding.

Mutual respect encourages open communication between teachers and pupils. When both parties feel valued and respected, they are more likely to engage in meaningful discussions and express their thoughts and concerns openly. This open dialogue cultivates a sense of trust and understanding within the classroom.

When teachers and pupils demonstrate mutual respect, it sets a positive example for behaviour within the learning environment. Students are more likely to exhibit respectful behaviour towards their peers when they observe respectful interactions between their teachers and themselves.

Mutual respect fosters empathy and understanding between teachers and pupils. When both parties acknowledge each other's perspectives and experiences, it promotes empathy and a deeper understanding of each other's challenges and strengths.

Chapter 31

'You're kept young'- Ms N

Nowadays, people spend hundreds of pounds of their hard-earned wages on beauty treatments, remedies and jiggery-pokery to stay young, or at least give the appearance of being young, however, I have the solution! Teaching.

Don't get me wrong, the late nights, the early morning commutes and the never-ending stack of bureaucracy will put more bags under your eyes than a plane can hold in its fuselage, but teaching can very much keep you young at heart.

One of the key reasons why teaching keeps individuals young at heart is the constant exposure to new ideas, concepts, and technologies. Educators are continuously learning and adapting to new teaching methods, technologies, and student needs. This ongoing process of learning and adaptation helps keep their minds sharp and agile, contributing to a youthful outlook on life. It is important for a teacher to remain current, not only in their specific subject area but also with the current culture within the year group you are teaching- this allows you to make the content within the lesson relevant to that of something the children will understand and relate to.

Teaching often involves fostering creativity and curiosity in students, which in turn influences educators themselves. By encouraging creativity and nurturing curiosity in their students, teachers also reignite their own sense of wonder and imagination. This continuous engagement with creativity and curiosity can have a rejuvenating effect on educators, keeping them youthful in spirit. As teachers, we are constantly needing to come up with new ways in which we can impart our knowledge to the next generation in an engaging manor, as a result this need breeds creativity within ourselves. This in turn is a quality within us that keeps us generally more youthful.

In the field of education, change is constant. From curriculum updates to technological advancements, educators are constantly embracing change and innovation. This adaptability not only enhances their professional skills but also keeps them open-minded and receptive to new ideas. Embracing change and innovation fosters a sense of vitality and enthusiasm, contributing to a youthful mindset among educators.

Successful teaching involves building meaningful connections with students, colleagues, and the community. These connections provide a sense of purpose and fulfilment, fostering a positive outlook on life. The interactions and relationships formed through teaching can bring joy, laughter, and a sense of belonging. This as a result can often keep teachers young at heart.

Most schools in the modern education system adopt the same mindset of 'lifelong learning'. As a result of this educators often advocate for the same 'lifelong learning' mindset, emphasising the importance of continuous personal and professional development. By embodying this philosophy, themselves, teachers stay intellectually engaged and curious about the world around them. This commitment to lifelong learning plays a significant role in keeping educators youthful in their approach to life.

Chapter 32

'You will make a difference'- Mr McG

On your worst day in school, it may be very difficult to actually believe, but when you stop and take a back step you realise that you will and do make a difference in the children you teach lives, as a result, it is vitally important that the difference you make is a positive one.

As a teacher, you are instrumental in fostering a love for learning and intellectual curiosity in your students. You provide guidance, support, and encouragement that can significantly impact a child's academic success. As Albert Einstein once said, 'It is the supreme art of the teacher to awaken joy in creative expression and knowledge.' The foundation you lay as a teacher is the fundamental building blocks for that of the future development of the child, and their success... no pressure then. We as an educators do it without even realising it. We teach fundamental basics that in two decades time, pupils will say 'I remember when Mr J taught me this....'

Furthermore, teachers have the ability to identify and nurture the unique talents and strengths of each student. By recognising individual learning styles and adapting their teaching methods accordingly, they can help students reach their full potential. Teachers serve as catalysts for this change by equipping students with the knowledge and skills they need to succeed academically.

In addition to academic growth, teachers also significantly impact the social and emotional development of their students. They create a supportive and inclusive classroom environment where children feel valued, respected, and empowered. Teachers have the ability to create positive emotional experiences that shape a child's self-esteem and confidence.

Moreover, teachers serve as role models for their students, demonstrating empathy, kindness, and resilience. By modelling positive behaviours and attitudes, they impart valuable life lessons that extend far beyond the classroom. Teachers guide students through challenges and setbacks, teaching them important lessons about perseverance and resilience.

Chapter 33

'Age Vs Stage'- Mrs D

It's a common misassumption by NQTs that all the children within your classroom are all the same as a result of their ages being the same- that is a catastrophic mistake to make and is one that will not bode well if you choose to make it.

As a teacher, it is crucial to recognise that not all pupils are at the same ability level, despite being the same age. Assuming that all students are at the same ability level solely based on their age can be detrimental to their learning and overall development.

Instead of focusing on age, it is essential to consider each student's individual stage of development and abilities. By doing so, educators can create a more inclusive and effective learning environment that caters to the diverse needs of their students.

Every student progress through various developmental stages at their own pace, not because they have hit an age milestone. These stages encompass cognitive, emotional, social, and physical development. Therefore, it is imperative for teachers to acknowledge and understand these differences in order to provide appropriate support and challenges for each student. By recognising individual developmental stages, educators can tailor their teaching methods to meet the specific needs of their students, fostering a more conducive learning environment.

While age may serve as a general guideline for academic expectations, for example, 'by year 9, a pupils should have the reading age of a 14-year-old'. Age should not be the sole determinant of a student's abilities or limitations. Each student's unique experiences, background, and individual growth trajectory contribute to their current stage of development. Therefore, assuming that all students of the same age have identical abilities overlooks the rich diversity within the classroom.

Acknowledging these differences allows teachers to implement differentiated instruction strategies that cater to individual strengths and areas for improvement.

Differentiated instruction involves tailoring teaching methods and content to accommodate the diverse learning needs within a classroom. By recognising that students are at different stages of development, educators can adjust their instructional approaches to ensure that each student is appropriately challenged and supported. This approach promotes inclusivity and equity in education by acknowledging and valuing the unique abilities of each student.

As Maya Angelou eloquently put it, 'We delight in the beauty of the butterfly but rarely admit the changes it has gone through to achieve that beauty.' This quote serves as a powerful reminder that each student undergoes their own journey of growth and development. It emphasises the importance of recognising individual progress and stages rather than making assumptions based solely on external factors such as age.

As a teacher, it is essential to move beyond assumptions based on age and instead focus on understanding each student's unique developmental stage. By recognising individual abilities and tailoring instruction accordingly, educators can create an inclusive learning environment that nurtures the diverse talents and potential within their classroom.

Chapter 34

'Don't plan a lesson that 100% relies on the pupils doing their homework'- Mr P

In the realm of education, teachers are constantly seeking ways to engage their students and facilitate effective learning. One common analogy often used to illustrate the importance of diverse learning strategies is the idea that a teacher should not plan a lesson that relies entirely on students completing their homework.

The analogy of not planning a lesson that depends on students completing their homework highlights the potential limitations of relying solely on one aspect of learning. Homework, while an essential part of a student's education, may not be the best indicator of their understanding or readiness for a particular lesson. Some students may struggle with completing homework assignments due to external factors such as family circumstances, health issues, or learning difficulties. By relying solely on homework completion, teachers risk overlooking these students and failing to provide the necessary support they need to succeed.

To combat the limitations of relying on homework, educators should incorporate diverse learning strategies into their lesson plans. This approach involves using a variety of teaching methods and resources to cater to different learning styles and abilities. For example, teachers can use visual aids, hands-on activities, group discussions, and individual work to engage students and promote understanding, as opposed to planning a lesson based around the idea of reviewing, or marking a homework that was previously set. By offering multiple pathways to learning, teachers can ensure that all students have the opportunity to succeed, regardless of their individual circumstances or learning preferences.

Incorporating diverse learning strategies into lesson plans offers numerous benefits for both students and teachers. Firstly, it promotes a more inclusive learning environment where all students feel valued and supported. Secondly, it allows teachers to better understand their students' strengths and weaknesses, enabling them to provide targeted feedback and support. Finally, it fosters a growth mindset in students, encouraging them to take ownership of their learning and develop resilience in the face of challenges.

To effectively implement diverse learning strategies, teachers should begin by assessing their students' individual needs and learning preferences. This can be done through informal conversations, observations, and formal assessments. Once teachers have a better understanding of their students, they can begin to design lessons that cater to these needs. This may involve using a variety of teaching methods, providing additional resources or support, and encouraging collaboration and peer-to-peer learning.

The analogy of not planning a lesson that relies entirely on students completing their homework serves as a powerful reminder of the importance of diverse learning strategies in education. By offering multiple pathways to learning, teachers can ensure that all students have the opportunity to succeed, regardless of their individual circumstances or learning preferences. By incorporating diverse learning strategies into lesson plans, educators can create a more inclusive and effective learning environment that fosters growth, resilience, and a love of learning in their students.

Chapter 35

'Learn as much from the children as they do you'-
Ms T

At the time of reading, I have been teaching for three years, and I can safely say in that time, I have been taught equally as much as much as I have taught.

The idea that a pupil or a group of pupils can teach a teacher as much as the teacher will teach them is a concept that has gained traction in educational circles, so much so that it is a common dissertation topic at university. This idea is based on the understanding that learning is a two-way street, where both teachers and pupils can benefit from the exchange of ideas, perspectives, and knowledge.

The concept aligns with the mindset that 'every day is a school day,' which emphasises the continuous nature of learning and the importance of being open to new ideas and experiences.

At the heart of this concept is the recognition that pupils bring unique perspectives, experiences, and knowledge to the classroom. They may have insights, questions, or ideas that challenge the teacher's assumptions, broaden their perspective, or deepen their understanding of a subject. By listening to and engaging with their pupils, teachers can learn new ways of approaching a topic, new strategies for teaching, and new insights into their own practice.

For example, a Geography teacher may be teaching a topic on local rural areas and ask their pupils to research and present on a particular aspect of the community's past. During the presentations, one pupil may share a story or artifact that the teacher had never heard of before, leading to a richer and more nuanced understanding of the community's history. In this way, the pupil has taught the teacher something new and valuable.

Similarly, teachers can also learn from their pupils by observing their learning styles, interests, and challenges. By paying attention to how their pupils engage with material, teachers can identify areas where they may need to adjust their teaching approach or provide additional support. For example, if a pupil is struggling with a particular concept, the teacher may need to find new ways to explain it or provide additional resources to help the pupil understand. By doing so, the teacher is not only helping the pupil but also learning more about effective teaching strategies.

Moreover, this symbiotic learning relationship can also foster a culture of curiosity and inquiry in the classroom. When teachers are open to learning from their pupils, they model a growth mindset and demonstrate the value of continuous learning. This can inspire pupils to ask questions, explore new ideas, and take ownership of their own learning.

For instance, a teacher may invite pupils to share their interests or passions and then incorporate those topics into the curriculum. By doing so, the teacher is not only engaging pupils in meaningful learning but also demonstrating a willingness to learn alongside them. This approach can create a sense of excitement and engagement in the classroom and help pupils see themselves as active contributors to their own education.

A pupil or a group of pupils can teach a teacher as much as the teacher will teach them is an important one that recognises the value of diverse perspectives, continuous learning, and collaboration in the classroom.

By embracing this mindset, teachers can create dynamic and engaging learning environments where everyone has something to contribute and something to learn. Every day truly is a learning day for both teachers and pupils alike.

Period 3

Chapter 36

'No sleep on results day-eve'- Mrs C

Potentially without realising it, you invest a lot of your time, heart and soul into your classes- especially your exam ones. As a result, the night before the results day, you will not rest. The children more than likely will have it not cost a thought, but you as a teacher understand the significance of what the next day has to bring, as a result it makes you- uneasy, to say the least.

The day before results day can be described as an emotional rollercoaster for teachers. While everyone is different and some teachers may not be too bothered about the revelation of results, most teachers I have met in my time are very much bothered. It is a time when they reflect on the journey they have taken with their students throughout the academic year. The investment of time, energy, and dedication to impart knowledge and support their students in reaching their potential is at the forefront of their minds. The emotional investment in each student's success can lead to a sense of personal responsibility and concern for their well-being.

Teachers often find themselves reflecting on the immense effort and commitment they have put into preparing their students for this moment. The countless hours spent planning lessons, providing extra support, and offering guidance all contribute to the weight of responsibility felt by teachers on the eve of results day. The desire to see their students succeed and achieve their goals is a driving force behind this unwavering commitment.

It is important to understand that if you do teach exam classes, around the time of results day, anticipation and anxiety are common emotions experienced by teachers as they await the unveiling of their students' results. The anticipation stems from a genuine interest in seeing the fruits of their labour come to fruition. However, this anticipation is often accompanied by anxiety, as teachers grapple with concerns about how their students will receive their results and how they will cope with the outcomes.

One of the most challenging aspects for teachers on the day before results day is recognising that not all students will share the same level of concern or investment in their academic outcomes. While some students may be filled with nervous energy and anticipation, others may appear indifferent or nonchalant about the impending results. This stark contrast in reactions can be perplexing for teachers who have invested so much in nurturing their students' growth and success.

During these emotions, teachers often find themselves making final preparations for results day. This may involve reviewing individual student performances, preparing to offer support and guidance based on different outcomes, and ensuring that they are emotionally equipped to handle any range of student reactions. In an essence, overthinking, over worrying and unintentionally thinking 'what if...'

The day before results day is a poignant time for teachers as they grapple with a myriad of emotions ranging from pride and anticipation to anxiety and concern. Their unwavering commitment to their students' success is evident in the weight they carry on this day. Despite the varying reactions from students, good teachers continue to stand as pillars of support, ready to guide and nurture each student through whatever outcome awaits them.

The most important thing to bear in mind is that despite the outcome of the results, you are there to support those children in whatever way you can- in that moment, if the results are poor, or not how you intended, you need to put your personal feelings aside and be the pillar of support for the child in question.

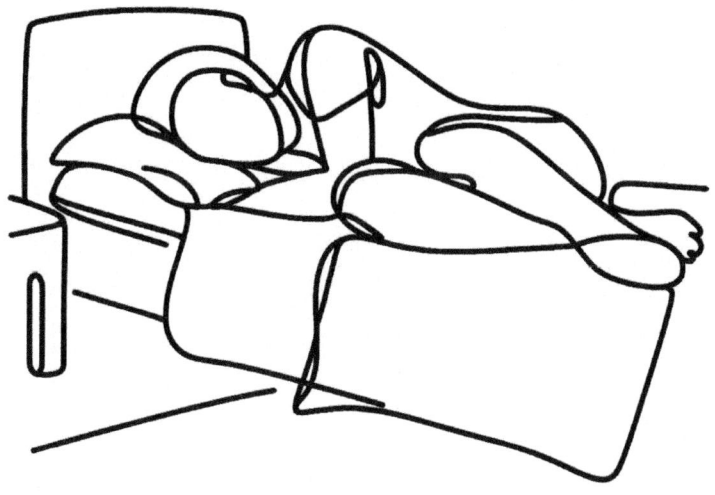

Chapter 37

'Exam results don't define the teacher'- Mr H

Picture the scene, you spend two years tirelessly working preparing an exam class for their exam, the day comes, and your heart is in your mouth, watching the clock tick by as they are in the exam hall– after that you patiently wait from May to August for the results... and...some pupils fail... does that make you a failure of a teacher? No, of course not!

As educators, we often can find ourselves in a position where our students' exam results become a reflection of our teaching abilities, it's almost like they are our personal results.

While it is essential to strive for excellence in our profession, it is crucial to remember that the outcomes of these assessments do not solely define us as teachers.

Examinations serve as a means to evaluate students' understanding of the subject matter and their ability to apply their knowledge in a structured setting. They provide valuable feedback for both students and teachers, allowing for targeted improvements in learning and teaching methods. However, it is essential to recognise that exams are just one aspect of a student's educational journey and should not be the sole determinant of their success or our effectiveness as educators.

To ensure that we do not solely rely on exam results to measure our success as teachers, we must shift our focus to the process of teaching and learning, and what that can tell us, as opposed to one cold hard raw fact, exam results. When thinking about teaching and learning we should consider,

Setting clear learning objectives: Which establishes specific, measurable, achievable, relevant, and time-bound (SMART) goals for our students helps create a roadmap for their academic growth.

Providing diverse teaching methods: Catering to different learning styles and preferences enables students to engage with the material more effectively, ultimately enhancing their understanding and retention of knowledge.

Encouraging active participation: Fostering an inclusive classroom environment where students feel comfortable asking questions, sharing ideas, and collaborating with their peers promotes a growth mindset.

Offering constructive feedback: Regularly providing meaningful feedback on students' progress allows them to identify areas for improvement and make necessary adjustments.

As teachers, we can help our students develop resilience and coping mechanisms to deal with the pressures associated with exams. We can do this though;

Modelling a growth mindset: Demonstrating that challenges are opportunities for growth and learning can inspire students to persevere through difficulties.

Teaching stress management techniques: Introducing relaxation exercises, time management strategies, and positive self-talk can help students manage exam-related stress.

Promoting a growth mindset: Encouraging students to view setbacks as opportunities for growth and learning can help them develop resilience in the face of challenges.

Imagine a tree, representing a student, bearing fruits, symbolising their exam results. While the fruits are essential for the tree's survival and growth, they are not the only aspect that defines the tree. The tree's trunk, branches, and leaves also contribute to its overall health and beauty. Similarly, a student's exam results are crucial, but their personal growth, character development, and life skills are equally significant. As teachers, we must nurture the entire tree, not just its fruits.

As educators, it is natural to feel a sense of pride and accomplishment when our students excel in exams. However, it is crucial to remember that our worth as teachers should not be solely determined by these outcomes. By focusing on the process of teaching and learning, building resilience in our students, and embracing a holistic approach to education, we can ensure that we are doing our best for our pupils while maintaining a healthy perspective on our professional identity. As teachers, we must recognise that exam results do not solely define our success or our students' potential. By adopting a holistic approach to education, focusing on the process of teaching and learning, and fostering resilience in our students, we can ensure that we are doing our best for them while maintaining a balanced perspective on our roles as educators.

Chapter 38

'Tutoring is key'- Mrs S

Tutoring plays a crucial role in the professional development of teachers, as it offers numerous benefits that extend beyond just fostering a positive relationship with students.

Tutoring provides teachers with an opportunity to establish a more personal connection with individuals. This one-on-one interaction allows them to understand each student's learning style, strengths, and weaknesses, which can be instrumental in tailoring teaching methods to cater to individual needs. As a result, teachers can create a more inclusive and supportive learning environment, fostering better academic performance and overall student satisfaction.

Through tutoring, teachers can refine their teaching skills by identifying areas where they need improvement. This process involves observing students' reactions to different teaching techniques, understanding their learning patterns, and adapting their approach accordingly. By doing so, teachers can enhance their communication skills, become more patient, and develop a better understanding of how to motivate and engage students.

Tutoring sessions often involve discussing exam content, which helps teachers stay updated on the latest developments in their subject area. This continuous engagement with the material ensures that their knowledge remains fresh and relevant. Moreover, tutoring allows teachers to identify any gaps in their understanding of the subject matter, prompting them to conduct further research and expand their knowledge base.

As teachers assist students in understanding complex concepts, they are also exposed to new perspectives and ways of thinking about the subject matter. This process of learning through teaching can lead to a deeper understanding of the subject, as well as the development of new ideas and insights. Consequently, teachers can enhance their subject knowledge and become more effective educators.

Not only this but tutoring serves as an essential tool for professional development, as it encourages teachers to reflect on their teaching practices and identify areas for improvement. This self-evaluation process can lead to the adoption of new teaching strategies, increased confidence in their abilities, and a stronger sense of professional identity.

By successfully guiding students through challenging concepts and exam content, teachers can build their confidence in their subject knowledge and teaching abilities. This increased self-assurance can translate into more effective classroom management, better communication with students, and a more engaging teaching style.

Tutoring fosters a culture of lifelong learning among teachers, which is handy considering most schools nowadays adopt the mindset of 'lifelong learning' as their school aim or vision. This is because it encourages teachers to stay updated on the latest developments in their subject area and teaching methodologies. This commitment to continuous learning not only benefits the teachers themselves but also has a positive impact on their students, as they witness their teachers' passion for knowledge and growth.

Tutoring plays a vital role in the professional development of teachers by enhancing their teaching skills, keeping their understanding of exam content fresh, and fostering a lifelong commitment to learning. By engaging in tutoring sessions, teachers can create a more inclusive and supportive learning environment, ultimately leading to better academic performance and overall student satisfaction.

Chapter 39

'Always have a spare pen with you on exam day'-
Mrs McK

In modern times, it is more likely that a student brings their brand-new top of the range recently released phone, smart watch and best pair of black trainers to an exam rather than the appropriate stationary needed to complete it.

While the title of this chapter specifically outlines bringing a spare pen, I think the message broadly spoken by Mrs McK, is that teachers need to be ready to cater for all needs of the children, not just academically but also in terms of stationary etc. No day is more important for a teacher to do this, than on exam days- simply because, one thing you can rely on, is that there will be at least one pupil, whose one thing they can rely on... is you.

A well-practiced and capable teacher understands that their role goes beyond just imparting academic knowledge to children. Teachers should also be there to provide necessary tools and support for the holistic development of the child, including stationary or apparatus when needed. While it is essential for teachers to equip students with the academic tools they require, it is equally important to address other needs that may arise.

In a classroom setting, there may be instances where a student takes advantage of the teacher's provision of stationary or apparatus. This can manifest in behaviours where a student constantly asks for items or misuses the resources provided. In such cases, teachers may need to adopt strategies during class time to manage these situations effectively. For example, implementing a system where students exchange personal items like phones for necessary tools like pens can help maintain discipline and teach responsibility. They can then receive their mobile back safely, when the apparatus they borrowed is returned safely. Pupils generally hate this, because they are usually surgically attached to their mobiles, so after a sustained period of adopting this strategy, you will find, the offending pupil will start bringing the apparatus needed rather than asking for yours. Such is the power of their attachment to their phone.

One crucial aspect of being a forward-thinking and prepared teacher is ensuring that students have access to essential tools during critical times, such as exam days. It is imperative for teachers to anticipate the needs of their students and provide additional stationary or resources to support them during exams. By being proactive and ensuring that every student is adequately equipped, teachers can create a conducive environment for academic success.

A good teacher recognises the importance of providing more than just academic tools for children. By offering support in various forms, including stationary or apparatus, when necessary, teachers can cater to the diverse needs of their students.

While challenges may arise, such as dealing with extreme cases of dependency on provided resources, effective strategies can be implemented to address these issues. Ultimately, by being forward-thinking and prepared, teachers can create a nurturing learning environment that fosters growth and success for all students.

Break

Chapter 40

'Do your duty!'- Mr McC

Fulfilling your assigned duty as a teacher is not just a task on your to-do list (as we have established, a never-ending to-do list), it is a crucial component of maintaining the smooth operation of a school environment.

By actively engaging in your duties, you not only demonstrate your commitment to being a team player but also contribute to the overall cohesiveness of the school community.

One of the key benefits of fulfilling your duties is the ability to address and prevent poor behaviour during unstructured times, such as transitions between classes or during breaks- as simple as standing in the doorway of your classroom during these times will massively help with crowd control and overall demeanour of the pupils.

When you consistently fulfil your assigned duties, you establish yourself as a reliable and responsible member of the school staff, to which the principal will highly appreciate. Your active participation in these tasks not only supports the efficient functioning of daily operations but also sets a positive example for students and colleagues alike. It showcases your dedication to creating a safe and orderly learning environment where everyone can thrive.

On the contrary, neglecting or dismissing your assigned duty even once can have significant consequences. The moment you decide to skip your duty or think that it will be 'fine' to do so, you open the door for potential disruptions or incidents to occur. This lapse in responsibility can lead to chaos, confusion, and even safety concerns within the school setting. It is essential to understand that every task, no matter how small it may seem, plays a vital role in upholding the standards and expectations of the educational institution. You can guarantee, that the one time that you neglect to do your duty, is when something drastic is going to happen, and then it will be you in the principal's office being asked why you weren't there...

In the words of a certain teenage spider superhero: 'With great power comes great responsibility.' As educators, we hold the power to influence and shape young minds, and with that power comes the responsibility to fulfil our duties diligently and conscientiously, both inside the classroom and outside of it as well. Fulfilling your assigned duty as a teacher is not just about completing a task; it is about upholding your commitment to your role in the school community. By actively engaging in your responsibilities, you contribute to a positive and structured learning environment while demonstrating professionalism and dedication to your profession.

Chapter 41

'Make the most of the time you get'- Miss O

As a teacher, time is a precious commodity, you hardly have time to count to ten or take a bathroom break without being interrupted. The demands of the profession often leave educators with limited free time during the school day. However, it is crucial for teachers to make the most of the little time they do have available, whether it be during breaks, lunch, or free periods. Maximising these moments can greatly impact productivity and overall well-being.

During short breaks throughout the day, teachers can benefit from taking a moment to recharge and refocus. Whether it's grabbing a quick snack, engaging in light conversation with colleagues, or simply taking a few deep breaths, these brief interludes can help alleviate stress and improve mental clarity. I have found that many teachers adopt the same approach to how they take their breaks. Initially, at the start of the year, everyone likes to socialise, catching up on gossip, scandal and banter they have missed out on over the summer period. However, as the year goes on, and the school becomes increasingly more busy– you find the teachers who did once like to socialise in the early stages of the year, now prefer to take time to themselves to increase their energy levels as opposed to draining their social battery. Taking advantage of these moments can lead to increased energy levels and improved focus when returning to teaching responsibilities.

Lunchtime provides teachers with a slightly longer period to regroup and prepare for the remainder of the day. This time can be used not only for nourishment but also for productive tasks such as planning lessons, grading assignments, or collaborating with fellow educators. By using lunchtime effectively, teachers can enhance their efficiency and effectiveness in the classroom.

In a busy school setting free periods are like gold dust. As I have previously outlined, keeping on the good side of the head of cover will allow you to ensure your free periods mostly stay as that, YOUR free periods. Free periods are valuable opportunities for teachers to tackle tasks that require more focused attention. Whether it's lesson planning, marking tests, attending professional development sessions, or organising classroom materials, free periods offer uninterrupted time to accomplish important work. By prioritising tasks during free periods, teachers can make significant progress on their responsibilities and feel more prepared for upcoming lessons.

Samuel F. Pickering Jr, the fella who 'John Keating' from Dead Poets Society was based upon once said; 'Time is a teacher's most valuable resource. How we choose to spend our free moments can greatly impact our effectiveness in the classroom.' Pickering underscored the importance of utilising every available minute wisely as a teacher. Making the most of free time as a teacher is essential for maintaining productivity, managing workload effectively, and fostering personal well-being. By strategically using breaks, lunchtime, and free periods, educators can optimise their time and ultimately enhance their teaching practice.

You as an educator is sole responsible for how you chose to spend your time, but make sure you do so wisely.

Chapter 42

'Find your group' - Ms C

This entire chapter is going to sound like it was written by a child on the playground talking about his friends, but the simple fact of the matter is that in a school setting, it is imperative that we find a body of people, whom you relate to and can get along with- your group.

Teaching can be a challenging profession, and having a support system is crucial. We all know that teaching is not just about imparting knowledge; it's also about emotional support for students. But who supports the teachers? That's where having a group of colleagues or friends comes in handy. When teachers socialise and bond with others, they have an outlet to share their challenges, seek advice, and receive emotional support. It can be therapeutic to have someone who understands the unique struggles of being an educator. This is a unique position where I believe if you aren't a teacher, you don't understand the struggles of a teacher- so having someone there who does, is vital to your ability to vent effectively.

Socialising with other teachers can also lead to professional growth. By engaging in conversations with peers, attending workshops, or participating in professional development activities together, teachers can exchange ideas, learn new teaching strategies, and stay updated on the latest trends in education. Building relationships with other educators can inspire creativity and innovation in the classroom.

However, let's be real here, socialising with other teachers isn't only just a way to professionally develop. It is also a way to vent any agitations, frustrations and aggrievances out, be that with the boss, the pupils or whomever, having a solid body of friends you know you can vent to without any blow back is hugely valued.

Teaching is not a solitary profession; it requires collaboration and teamwork. When teachers socialise and form bonds with their colleagues, they are more likely to collaborate on projects, share resources, and work together to create a positive learning environment for students. A strong sense of camaraderie among teachers can lead to better outcomes for both educators and students. Just as recently as last year, I collaborated with another teacher to create the 'Great Boat Race' where pupils in year 8 combined Science and Technology skills to make boys float across a paddling pool and reach the other side first. It culminated in a fun afternoon in the sunshine playing with toy boats. Although considering I came last in the race, I suspect foul play... I'm not bitter as you can tell.

Teaching can be emotionally draining, leading to burnout if not managed properly. By socialising and building relationships with others, teachers can prevent feelings of isolation and burnout. Having a supportive network can help teachers recharge, stay motivated, and find joy in their profession. It's crucial for teachers not to outcast themselves but instead find a group of people whom they can relate to and bond with. Socialising and building relationships not only provide emotional support but also foster professional growth, collaboration, teamwork, and help prevent burnout. So go ahead, connect with your fellow educators – it's beneficial for both you and your students!

Chapter 43

'Make yourself a supply rota' - Mr J

If you're lucky enough like I am, you will hopefully find a group of people who share the same interests as you. If you're even more lucky, someone within that group will be a 'mother hen' type figure and provide all the supplies you need for a break or lunch time catch up. Milk, tea bags, sugar... life is great! Until that person disappears for a while.

That happened us, our mother hen went away to become a literal mother- she went to look after her baby at the house rather the babies with teaching degrees she looked after in the school. You can't exactly blame her... How we got around this situation however was simple, for the 6 months she was off, we had black tea, reused the bags so that they wouldn't run out and stirred them with the handle of a butter knife. We made the most of what we could in dire times, resorting to using what we could to make ends meet. I viewed it as Bear Grylls-esque. Others viewed it as using a 150mm steel rule as a knife to butter a scone....

Not exactly the luxury we were used to. It took us all too long to realise that the solution to our new poverty breaks was actually a supply rota. Sounds obvious when you think about it...

Having a supply rota in place might seem like a trivial matter, but it can make a significant difference in the daily lives of coffee craving teachers. By establishing a clear schedule for restocking essentials like milk, sugar, tea bags, and coffee, you ensure that these items are always available when needed. This simple act can boost morale and productivity by preventing unnecessary disruptions and ensuring that employees can enjoy their breaks without any hiccups.

Picture this: it's mid-morning, and you're craving a hot cup of tea to keep you going. You head to the break room, only to find that there's no milk left. Why? Now you have to trek back to your classroom or even worse, venture outside to get some milk from a nearby shop. Not only does this waste time, but it also disrupts your workflow and leaves you feeling annoyed. By implementing a supply rota, you eliminate these unnecessary frustrations and create a more seamless experience for everyone in the office.

A supply rota isn't just about ensuring that there's always milk and sugar available; it's also about fostering a sense of teamwork and responsibility among employees. When everyone takes turns restocking the break room supplies according to the rota, it instils a culture of shared ownership and accountability. This simple task can promote collaboration and unity within the team, showing that everyone plays a part in creating a positive work environment.

Creating a supply rota for the break room may seem like a small detail, but its impact shouldn't be underestimated. By ensuring that essentials are consistently restocked, you not only avoid unnecessary frustrations but also promote teamwork and responsibility among employees. So next time you reach for that cup of coffee, remember the importance of having a well-organised supply rota in place.

Chapter 44

'Outside of school' - Mr B

Socialising with colleagues outside of work, such as playing golf together, going walks or even holidays can significantly impact the dynamics within a team. This informal setting allows for deeper connections to form, fostering a sense of community and closeness among staff members. When individuals engage in activities like golfing together, they have the opportunity to bond over shared interests and experiences, which can strengthen their relationships beyond the confines of the workplace.

Engaging in social activities outside of work promotes a sense of community within the team. By spending time together in a more relaxed environment, colleagues can get to know each other on a personal level, building trust and camaraderie. This sense of community can lead to improved communication, collaboration, and overall morale within the group. For example, imagine a group of teachers who regularly meet up to play golf on weekends. Through these outings, they not only enjoy a fun activity together but also have the chance to discuss work-related matters in a more casual setting. This informal interaction can strengthen their professional relationships and create a supportive network within the school community.

Socialising outside of work can also help foster closeness among staff members. When individuals take the time to connect outside of their professional roles, they develop a deeper understanding of each other's personalities and interests. This closeness can lead to increased empathy, respect, and collaboration within the team.

For instance, consider a scenario where colleagues organise regular golf outings as a way to unwind and relax together. These shared experiences create lasting memories and inside jokes that contribute to a more cohesive team dynamic. As a result, staff members are more likely to support each other both professionally and personally.

On the flip side, failing to socialise with colleagues outside of work can potentially lead to feelings of alienation or isolation within the team. When individuals do not participate in group activities or social gatherings, they may miss out on valuable opportunities to connect with their peers. This lack of engagement can create barriers between team members and hinder effective communication and collaboration.

Socialising with colleagues outside of work, whether through activities like playing golf or other shared interests, is essential for promoting a sense of community and closeness within a team. By fostering these connections, individuals can build stronger relationships, enhance teamwork, and create a supportive work environment.

Period 4

Chapter 45

'Stand at the door when letting the children into the room' – Ms B

Greeting students at the door as they enter the classroom is a practice that holds significant importance in establishing a positive and structured learning environment. While it may seem like a simple gesture, this act can have profound effects on the overall dynamics of the classroom.

By standing at the door and welcoming each student individually, teachers can set the tone for the lesson and create a sense of order right from the beginning. This small act helps in signalling to students that they are entering a space where respect, discipline, and attentiveness are valued. It also helps in minimising disruptions as students transition from the hallway to the classroom setting.

Greeting students at the door provides teachers with an opportunity to connect with each student on a personal level. It allows for brief interactions where teachers can inquire about their well-being, offer words of encouragement, or address any immediate concerns. These interactions help in building rapport and trust between teachers and students, which is essential for effective teaching and learning.

Consistency is key in education, and greeting students at the door establishes a routine that students can rely on. When this practice is consistently followed, it becomes ingrained in the daily flow of the classroom, creating a sense of predictability and stability for students. This routine can help in reducing anxiety and uncertainty, especially for students who thrive in structured environments.

While greeting students at the door may seem like a minor aspect of teaching, its impact on classroom management, student-teacher relationships, and overall learning environment should not be underestimated. By incorporating this simple practice into their daily routine, teachers can set a positive tone for learning and create a welcoming atmosphere that fosters student engagement and success.

Chapter 46

'It is important to have a good work ethic' – Mr K

In the realm of education, having a strong work ethic is paramount for teachers. A good work ethic not only benefits the teacher themselves but also greatly impacts the students they teach.

In modern times, the prevalence of a strong work ethic among teachers seems to be dwindling, making it even more crucial for those who uphold it to stand out.

One of the key aspects of a good work ethic for teachers is dedication and commitment to their profession. Teachers who are dedicated to their students and committed to providing quality education go above and beyond in their roles. This dedication often translates into better student outcomes and overall classroom success.

Teachers with a strong work ethic serve as role models for their students. By demonstrating hard work, perseverance, and a commitment to excellence, they instil these values in their students as well. Students are more likely to respect and emulate teachers who exhibit a strong work ethic.

For Newly Qualified Teachers (NQTs), maintaining a strong work ethic is crucial for standing out in a competitive field. With many new teachers entering the profession each year, those who demonstrate exceptional dedication and commitment through their work ethic are more likely to succeed and advance in their careers.

The late football legend Pele once said, 'Success is no accident. It is hard work, perseverance, learning, studying, sacrifice, and most of all, love of what you are doing or learning to do'. While teaching isn't equivalent to playing football in the World Cup final, regardless of the job, a person should love all that they do and give their all to their job.

Having a good work ethic as a teacher is essential not only for personal success but also for the success of students. In today's educational landscape where dedication and commitment can sometimes be lacking, teachers who maintain a strong work ethic have the opportunity to truly make a difference in the lives of their students.

Chapter 47

'Know your learning types' — Miss W

As a teacher, understanding the various learning types of your pupils is crucial for creating an inclusive and effective learning environment. Every student is unique, and their preferred learning style can significantly impact how they process information, engage with the material, and ultimately succeed in their academic pursuits. By identifying and accommodating different learning styles, educators can better cater to the diverse needs of their students and enhance overall learning outcomes.

Visual Learners

Visual learners prefer to process information through visual aids such as charts, diagrams, and videos. These students benefit from colourful presentations, visual demonstrations, and graphic organisers. For example, when teaching a lesson on photosynthesis, incorporating diagrams illustrating the process can greatly assist visual learners in grasping the concept.

Auditory Learners

Auditory learners learn best through listening and verbal instruction. These students thrive in discussions, lectures, and audio recordings. To support auditory learners, teachers can incorporate group discussions, read-aloud sessions, and educational podcasts into their lesson plans. When teaching a historical event like the American Revolution, engaging auditory learners through storytelling or listening to historical speeches can be highly effective.

Kinaesthetic Learners

kinaesthetic learners learn by doing and engaging in hands-on activities. These students excel in labs, experiments, role-playing exercises, and other interactive tasks. For example, when teaching a science lesson on friction, providing kinaesthetic learners with materials to build simple machines or conduct experiments can deepen their understanding of the concept.

Tactile Learners

Tactile learners learn best through touch and physical interaction. These students benefit from manipulatives, tactile materials, and sensory experiences. For instance, when teaching geometry concepts like angles and shapes, tactile learners can benefit from using geometric shapes to physically explore and manipulate the properties of different figures.

By recognising and accommodating these various learning styles in the classroom, teachers can create a more inclusive and engaging learning environment that caters to the diverse needs of all students. Differentiating instruction based on learning types not only enhances student comprehension but also fosters a positive attitude towards learning and promotes academic success for all learners.

Chapter 48

'You need to have thick skin' — Ms McC

In a school environment, teachers are often subjected to various comments and jokes from students and even colleagues. I honestly think I could write a book, based on the jokes I've received since graduating... and that's just from my colleagues!

To maintain a positive and productive atmosphere, it is crucial for educators to develop thick skin. This means not taking every remark personally and understanding that most of these comments are just jokes or casual banter.

Children in the classroom may comment on a teacher's appearance, actions, or decisions. They might do this behind the teacher's back in a group of them, or directly to your face– the latter of which I would highly suggest gets nipped in the bud immediately. It is also paramount to remember that you are the adult and professional in the room, so absolutely should you not stoop to that of the level of a teenager and retaliate in the same manner.

This would negate any control of the class you have and set an example and tone of approval towards this slanderous behaviour. If you set a precedent of encouraging this line of behaviour, you encourage the continuation of such going forward.

Similarly, in the staffroom, colleagues engage in light-hearted banter, where everyone is fair game for teasing. It could be on where you're from, your appearance, your work ethic, accent... anything. In such situations, it is essential to recognise that these comments do not define the teacher's worth or abilities. They are merely jokes, and the person making the comment likely does not mean any harm.

However as childish and as immature as it might seem, the fact of the matter is if the same person repeatedly targets with the same type of comment or joke, it may cross the line into bullying.

In these cases, you should not hesitate to seek help from the principal or vice principal, just as you would advise a pupil facing similar issues to go to their direct superior, their form teacher of head of year, you should do the same.

Teachers must cultivate thick skin to navigate the social dynamics of a school environment. By understanding that most comments are harmless jokes and addressing any potential bullying, educators can maintain a positive outlook and focus on their primary role: teaching and supporting students.

Chapter 49

'You'll have them when you can hold their attention' — Mr J

A good friend of mine once said 'You will have them when you can hold their attention', and for a long time I could never understand what he meant by that, surely as a teacher when you talk, they listen, and you have their attention? I mean, who wouldn't want to be fully engaged with some potential divider equations in Technology or the history of Berlin Wall in History, right?

However, I then realised that he wasn't referring to the moment of actually teaching where you'll know you have them if you can hold their attention. He in fact was referring to the moments that you aren't teaching, and how they behave during them.

In the realm of education and communication, there exists a profound concept that revolves around the ability to capture and maintain the attention of an audience, particularly children. This concept goes beyond merely teaching a lesson; it delves into the realm of influence and engagement. When you hold the attention of children to the extent that they remain focused even amidst interruptions like a ringing phone or external disturbances, you wield a powerful tool. It signifies that you have established a connection with your audience that transcends mere instruction.

Capturing and maintaining the attention of children, especially in environments prone to distractions, is an art form. It requires a delicate balance of engaging content, interactive delivery, and a genuine connection with the audience. When children are so engrossed in what you are presenting that they remain attentive despite external disruptions, it speaks volumes about your ability to command their focus and respect.

Having children engrossed in what you are presenting to them is a brilliant aspect of teaching to have in any regard, however, in a busy school where at any time the phone can ring, a teacher can walk in or even the fire bell can go– it's a brilliant insurance policy knowing that regardless of the attraction, the children will remain on task and focused on what you are dishing up to them.

Rory Sutherland, a renowned behavioural economist, author, and recent social media sensation, once stated, 'Attention is a resource—a person has only so much of it.' Which encapsulates the essence of capturing and maintaining attention, emphasising its value as a limited yet potent resource.

When children choose to invest their attention in your words and actions, even when faced with distractions, they are essentially placing their trust in you as a communicator and mentor. When children choose to keep their attention on you during moments of interruption or external disturbances, it signifies a deeper level of engagement and respect for your authority. It indicates that they value what you have to say and are willing to prioritise your message above other distractions. This level of uninterrupted engagement not only enhances the learning experience but also fosters a sense of mutual understanding and connection between the educator and the students.

Generally, the ability to hold children's attention even in the face of interruptions is a testament to effective communication, engaging content, and mutual respect. It signifies a strong bond between the educator and the students, where trust, influence, and learning thrive in an environment characterised by unwavering focus.

Period 5

Chapter 50

'Use your skills to contribute to the school community' — Ms C

JFK once said, 'One person can make a difference, and everyone should try', and I believe that this is a brilliant mindset to have in the school, we all can contribute. Being an active contributor to the school community as a teacher is crucial for fostering a positive and supportive educational environment.

Each individual has unique skills and talents that can benefit the school community in various ways. Whether it's organising extracurricular activities, baking treats for colleagues, or managing social media accounts, every contribution plays a significant role in enhancing the overall school experience.

By actively participating in the school community, teachers can create a supportive and inclusive environment for both students and colleagues. When teachers engage in activities outside of the classroom, such as coaching sports teams or leading clubs, they demonstrate their commitment to the holistic development of students. This involvement helps build strong relationships with students and fosters a sense of belonging within the school community.

Now I know what you're thinking, 'I have nothing to offer that a school would be interested in'. But as the former president of the United States of America said so poetically, every person should try and make that difference. Every teacher possesses unique skills and talents that can be utilised to enrich the school community. For example, a teacher who excels in baking can contribute by preparing treats for staff meetings or special events. Another teacher who is proficient in social media management can help promote school activities and events online, increasing engagement and awareness within the community. By leveraging these individual strengths, teachers can make valuable contributions that enhance the overall school experience.

Contributing to the school community encourages collaboration and teamwork among teachers, students, and staff members. When teachers actively participate in school events and initiatives, they set a positive example for students and demonstrate the importance of working together towards common goals. This collaborative spirit not only strengthens relationships within the school community but also fosters a sense of unity and shared purpose.

Contributing to the school community as a teacher is essential for creating a supportive environment, utilising individual skills, and promoting collaboration and teamwork. Every contribution, no matter how big or small, plays a vital role in enhancing the overall educational experience for everyone involved.

Chapter 51

'It's important to be media literate' — Mrs D

As a child, in my household, if anyone had a technology related issue, they handed their phone, laptop or whatever device it was to me. This wasn't because I was the technological version of Doctor Doo-Little, but more because of my presence in growing up in the digital age, meant that I usually knew what to do to fix the problem.

In today's digital age, being media literate is crucial for educators to effectively navigate the vast array of resources available and to enhance their teaching practices. Media literacy encompasses the ability to access, analyse, evaluate, and create media in various forms. As a teacher, developing media literacy skills not only benefits your own professional growth but also empowers you to better engage with students in a technology-driven world.

One of the primary advantages of being media literate as a teacher is the ability to access a wide range of educational resources online. From lesson plans and teaching materials to educational videos and interactive simulations, the internet offers a wealth of resources that can enrich classroom instruction. By honing your skills in navigating online platforms and discerning credible sources from misinformation, you can effectively leverage digital resources to enhance your teaching strategies.

Media literacy also plays a vital role in utilising software and technology tools to create engaging learning experiences for students. Proficiency in educational software applications allows teachers to design multimedia presentations, interactive quizzes, and virtual learning environments that cater to diverse learning styles. By staying abreast of technological advancements and understanding how to integrate digital tools into lesson plans, educators can foster a dynamic and interactive learning environment that resonates with today's tech-savvy students.

Furthermore, being media literate enables teachers to effectively communicate with parents through online platforms such as virtual parent-teacher conferences or digital newsletters. By harnessing digital communication tools, educators can keep parents informed about their child's progress, share important updates about school events, and solicit feedback on student performance. Establishing clear channels of communication through digital media fosters collaboration between teachers and parents, ultimately benefiting the overall academic success of students.

In conclusion, media literacy is an essential skill set for educators in the modern era. By embracing media literacy practices, teachers can harness the power of digital resources, software tools, and online communication platforms to enhance their teaching effectiveness and engage with students in innovative ways.

Chapter 52

'Wait for it...... Patience' – Mr F

Patience is a crucial characteristic for any teacher to possess. It allows educators to create a positive learning environment, build strong relationships with students, and effectively help students learn and grow.

Patience is essential for creating a positive learning environment where students feel comfortable making mistakes and asking questions. When teachers are patient, they are better able to respond calmly and supportively to student errors, which encourages students to take risks and try new things. This, in turn, leads to a more engaging and productive learning experience for all students.

For example, imagine a Maths teacher who becomes frustrated when a student struggles to solve a problem. The teacher may become impatient and raise their voice, causing the student to feel embarrassed and shut down. This negative experience can discourage the student from asking for help in the future and hinder their learning. On the other hand, if the teacher responds with patience and understanding, the student is more likely to feel supported and motivated to continue trying.

Patience also plays a key role in building strong relationships with students. When teachers are patient, they are better able to listen to students' concerns and needs, which helps to establish trust and respect. This strong foundation is essential for fostering open communication and creating a supportive learning community.

For example, consider an English teacher who has a student who is struggling to keep up with the reading assignments. Instead of becoming frustrated and assigning additional work as punishment, the teacher takes the time to understand the student's challenges and work with them to find a solution. This patient approach helps to build a positive relationship between the teacher and student, which can lead to increased engagement and academic success for the student.

Finally, patience is crucial for helping students learn and grow. When teachers are patient, they are better able to provide individualised instruction and support that meets the unique needs of each student. This personalised approach allows students to progress at their own pace and reach their full potential.

For example, imagine a music teacher who is working with a group of beginning violinists. Some students may pick up the instrument quickly, while others may struggle with the basics. A patient teacher will recognise that each student has their own learning style and will take the time to provide individualised instruction and support. This approach helps all students make progress and develop their skills over time.

In her book 'The Power of Patience in Teaching,' author Jessica Lahey explores the importance of patience in education and provides practical strategies for teachers to cultivate this essential skill. Lahey argues that 'patience is not only a virtue but also a practical tool that can help us be more effective teachers'. She provides numerous examples of how patience can improve classroom dynamics, build stronger relationships with students, and support student learning and growth. Lahey's book is a topical modern reference that highlights the significance of patience in teaching and offers valuable insights for educators at all levels.

Patience is an essential characteristic for any teacher to possess. It allows educators to create a positive learning environment, build strong relationships with students, and effectively help students learn and grow. By cultivating patience in the classroom, teachers can create a supportive learning community where all students feel valued, respected, and empowered to succeed.

Chapter 53

'Conflict resolution' – Ms M

A good and well-practised teacher is not just a teacher. We as educators are also, life coaches, motivator, entertainer, scheduler, organiser, reality checker, babysitters, first aiders but also, a mediator. Teachers are arguably the profession that deals with the highest level of conflict resolution. Honestly, if teachers were running the country, Brexit wouldn't be a word.

Conflict resolution skills are essential for teachers to effectively manage and maintain a positive learning environment within the classroom. Teachers often find themselves in situations where conflicts arise between students, and their ability to address and resolve these conflicts can significantly impact the overall classroom dynamics and student relationships.

When conflicts occur between students, it can disrupt the learning process and create a negative atmosphere in the classroom. Teachers with strong conflict resolution skills can address these issues promptly and effectively, ensuring that students feel safe, respected, and supported in their learning environment.

By actively resolving conflicts between students, teachers also have the opportunity to teach valuable social skills such as communication, empathy, and problem-solving. These skills are essential for students to navigate conflicts not only in the classroom but also in their future personal and professional lives.

Conflict resolution helps build a sense of community within the classroom by promoting understanding, cooperation, and mutual respect among students. When conflicts are resolved in a constructive manner, it strengthens the relationships between students and creates a more harmonious learning environment.

Conflict resolution skills are equally important for teachers when managing conflicts among staff members. As department heads, particularly that of subjects that have large amounts of teaching staff or technicians within; Technology, Art or Science for example, teachers must be able to address interpersonal conflicts among colleagues in a professional and impartial manner.

Resolving staff conflicts promptly can help maintain team cohesion and productivity within the school or educational organisation. When conflicts are left unresolved, they can escalate and negatively impact the overall work environment, leading to decreased morale and performance.

Teachers who demonstrate effective conflict resolution skills serve as role models for both students and colleagues. By handling conflicts with tact, empathy, and fairness, teachers set a positive example of how to manage disagreements constructively and promote a culture of respect and collaboration.

Conflict resolution skills are vital for teachers not only in managing conflicts between students but also in effectively addressing staff disputes. By cultivating these skills, teachers can create a positive learning environment, teach valuable social skills, foster community spirit, promote team cohesion, and set a positive example for others to follow.

Chapter 54

'You are an advocate for your school' — Mr P

Teachers play a crucial role not only in educating students but also in advocating for their schools. As a teacher you are a representative of the school.

Often, before going on a school trip, I, along with probably hundreds of other teachers within the academic year say the words, 'you are wearing the uniform, and when you do, you are representing the school'. In many ways teachers also have to hold themselves to such scrutiny. We are tagged with the name of the school in our day-to-day life and are a daily advocate for it.

Being an advocate for their school means actively supporting and promoting the school's mission, values, and goals. It involves speaking up for the needs of the school, its students, and the education system. Teachers who serve as advocates can make a significant impact on their school community and beyond.

One of the primary reasons why teachers should be advocates for their schools is to ensure that students receive the best possible education. Teachers are in a unique position to understand the needs and challenges that students face on a daily basis. By advocating for resources, support services, and policies that benefit students, teachers can help create a more conducive learning environment.

Teachers can also advocate for their school by supporting their colleagues. Collaboration among teachers is essential for creating a positive school culture and fostering professional growth. By advocating for opportunities for professional development, mentorship programs, and a supportive work environment, teachers can contribute to the overall success of their school.

Another important aspect of being an advocate for their school is engaging with parents and the community. Teachers can build strong partnerships with parents by keeping them informed about their child's progress, involving them in school activities, and addressing any concerns they may have. By fostering positive relationships with parents and community members, teachers can help create a sense of belonging and support for the school.

Being an advocate for their school is essential for teachers to create a positive impact on students, colleagues, parents, and the community. By actively promoting the values and goals of their school, teachers can contribute to a supportive learning environment that nurtures academic success and personal growth.

Period 6

Chapter 55

'Tidy Desk, Tidy Mind' – Mr J

In the realm of education, the idea that a tidy desk reflects a tidy mind has been a topic of discussion among teachers for quite some time- there is literally lectures, dissertations and philosophies based on this idea. The concept suggests that the state of one's physical workspace, particularly a teacher's desk, can have an impact on their mental clarity, organisation, and overall effectiveness in their role as an educator.

The notion of a tidy desk equating to a tidy mind can be traced back to early philosophies on organisation and productivity. Influential figures such as Leonardo da Vinci and Albert Einstein were known for maintaining organised workspaces, which some believe contributed to their creative thinking and problem-solving abilities. Now, if you look at the famous photo Einstein's desk, just after he died, you will not think for a second it was organised- but to him it was exactly that, he knew where everything was, exactly where it needed to be when he needed it to be.

From a psychological standpoint, the environment in which individuals work can influence their cognitive processes and emotional well-being. A cluttered desk may lead to feelings of overwhelm, distraction, and stress, whereas a tidy desk can promote focus, efficiency, and a sense of control.

In the context of teaching, having a tidy desk can also impact how educators are perceived by students, parents, and colleagues. A clean and organised workspace and classroom may convey professionalism, attention to detail, and dedication to their role as a teacher.

Practically speaking, a tidy desk can enhance productivity by reducing the time spent searching for materials, minimising distractions, and facilitating smoother workflow. Teachers who maintain an orderly workspace may find it easier to plan lessons, mark test, and engage with students effectively.

However, it is essential to acknowledge that not all educators subscribe to the belief that a tidy desk is synonymous with a tidy mind. Some teachers thrive in more chaotic environments and may feel stifled by overly neat surroundings. There is a particular maths teacher who comes to mind, over the space of a two-week period where on a few occasions I covered his form class while he was on paternity leave, I could not deal with the set-up of his desk and the location of documents and pages. Eventually I ended up taking his form class in my room as opposed to his.

However, that doesn't mean he or I was more or less capable at our jobs than the other. Personal preferences and individual working styles should also be taken into consideration when evaluating the impact of workspace organisation on teaching effectiveness.

While the concept of a tidy desk reflecting a tidy mind holds merit for many educators, its significance ultimately varies from person to person. Whether one's workspace is meticulously arranged or creatively disordered, what truly matters is finding an organisational system that supports one's teaching practice and fosters optimal performance in the classroom.

As a good rule of thumb, I tidy my desk at the end of every day, simply because you never know what the time, you're not at work will hold, and coming to work with a messy desk again after the fact is just one less stress or pressure that can be avoided.

Chapter 56

'Get yourself a routine, if you can' — Mrs H

Ok, I will admit it, in case you can't tell by the meticulous organisation, division, subdivision and structure of this book, I am a serial planner. It's how I structure my life in general, I plan my day the night before and stick to it the next day, and the cycle repeats that night. This, I believe is a good quality to have as a teacher, it allows us as educators to establish a routine within our day to day lives on the job.

Establishing a routine as a teacher is crucial for maintaining productivity, efficiency, and overall well-being. By following a set schedule, teachers can benefit in various ways that ultimately enhance their performance in the classroom.

One of the key advantages of having a routine as a teacher is the ability to plan effectively. When you have a consistent schedule, you can allocate specific time slots for lesson planning, marking, and other essential tasks. This structured approach allows you to stay organised and ensure that you are adequately prepared for each day, so you can't be caught out with the queue at the photocopier five minutes before your next class for example.

Having a routine helps teachers stay focused on their tasks and responsibilities. By eliminating decision fatigue associated with figuring out what to do next, teachers can direct their energy towards teaching and engaging with students. This increased focus leads to higher productivity levels and better outcomes in the classroom.

A routine provides structure to the day, which is especially important in a dynamic environment like a school. Knowing what to expect at different times of the day helps teachers manage their time efficiently and maintain a sense of order amidst the chaos that can sometimes arise in a classroom setting. Now, as we already have discussed, this isn't always possible, it's a school- a ever changing organism that will never have the same day twice, but it is better to be planned for what should happen than not be planned at all. Proactive rather than reactive.

When teachers adhere to a routine, they become more accountable for their actions and commitments. By setting specific goals and timelines for completing tasks, teachers hold themselves to a higher standard of performance. This accountability fosters professionalism and ensures that important responsibilities are not overlooked.

A good friend once shared their perspective on the benefits of having a routine as a teacher, saying, 'Knowing if I'm coming or going is the best thing as a teacher because it means I can plan to come and I can plan to go as well'. Now, knowing my friend and some of their antics, this is actually quite a wise comment, simply because it encapsulates the essence of how establishing a routine can bring clarity and purpose to the daily life of an educator.

Getting yourself into a routine as a teacher is essential for maximising efficiency, productivity, and overall job satisfaction.

By embracing structure and consistency in your daily activities, you can experience significant improvements in planning abilities, focus, day structure, and accountability.

Better to be planned and have it, than unplanned and need it, in my book... literally.

Chapter 57

'Early morning starts' – Mr D

When I first started in my current school, I lived approximately the same distance as the Kessel run, a journey that a certain space smuggler was able to transverse in 12 parsecs. The unfortunate part for me is I didn't have a Millennium Falcon to do my journey in, instead it took me about an hour and twenty minutes each way. As a result, I would leave my house at 10 to 7 every morning and arrive at the school at around 10 past 8, assuming there weren't any rural hold ups, like tractors or sheep.

A good friend of mine, always said I was mad leaving the house when I did and arriving when I did, but I believed it to be beneficial. That time in the morning before the pupils started to arrive allowed me to start my day with a buffer and give me a bit of breathing room to get organised for the day or grab a coffee.

As a teacher, how your day goes is determined very early on, so starting the school day off on the right foot is crucial for setting the tone for both you and your students.

One of the primary benefits of arriving at school early is the ability to get organised before the students arrive, as I've mentioned. This can include setting up the classroom, preparing materials for lessons, and reviewing lesson plans. By having extra time to get these tasks done, you can start the day feeling more prepared and less stressed. Additionally, if any unexpected issues arise, such as a technology malfunction or a missing supply, you will have time to address them before the students arrive.

Another benefit of arriving at school early is avoiding traffic. Depending on the location of the school and the time of day, traffic can significantly impact your commute. By leaving your house a bit earlier, you can avoid peak traffic hours and ensure that you arrive at school on time and calmly. This can help reduce stress and anxiety associated with being late or rushing to get to school. You simply can't predict what you might come across on your travels, be it tractors, sheep, roadworks- it could be anything, or god forbid, you could wake up, go outside and see that your car has a flat tyre, that's a hassle you don't need in the morning as is, but if you run a tight to the wire commute, it can essentially guarantee your lateness before you even attempt to make it on time. By leaving that bit earlier you give yourself that extra bit of breathing room.

Arriving at school early also provides opportunities to build relationships with colleagues and school staff. Whether it's catching up with a co-worker in the staff room or chatting with the school secretary, these interactions can help foster a positive and supportive work environment. Additionally, building relationships with colleagues can lead to collaborative opportunities and a sense of community within the school.

Finally, arriving at school early can provide personal time before the chaos of the day begins. Whether you use this time to grab a cup of coffee, take a walk around the school grounds, or simply sit and collect your thoughts, having this time to yourself can help you feel more cantered and focused when the students arrive. This personal time can also help reduce burnout and increase job satisfaction. I have been known to arrive to school early, put the feet up and watch a bit of a particular streaming service and unwind before the chaos ensues.

Arriving at school early can have numerous benefits for teachers. From getting organised to building relationships and taking personal time, this small change can have a significant impact on your overall well-being and job satisfaction. So, consider setting your alarm a bit earlier and enjoy the benefits of starting your day off on the right foot.

Chapter 58

'You can weaponise sub teachers' — Mr L

As a professional, we are encouraged where possible to not take any time off. However, on occasion this is unfortunately unavoidable, be it because of medical reasons, personal reasons or even school trips. When this happens, the school has two options. The first, they can utilise their present teaching staff on their already maxed out free periods and ask them to cover a period. This ends up meaning you've one teacher covering you for one period, and another teacher for the next and so on.

The second option is to employ a substitute teacher for the day and ask them to cover you from the start of the day to the end of the day, generally speaking, this is the better option. However, depending on how you prepare the day for those subs, you can either return to your classroom, everything neat and tidy, ready to pick up where they left off, or you could be coming into an educational version of the opening scene of 'Saving Private Ryan'. Now, which option you wish to have after returning from a day off is ultimately out of your control, however, what you can do, is help the sub in such a way that will ensure you have a smooth as silk return to school. You, through the use of the work you set can weaponise the sub.

As a teacher, your absence can disrupt the flow of learning in your classroom. However, by strategically preparing and supporting (or weaponising) the substitute teacher who covers for you, you can ensure a smooth day for both the substitute and your students.

When you empower a substitute teacher, you are equipping them with the tools and resources they need to succeed in managing your classroom. This includes providing detailed lesson plans, clear instructions on classroom procedures, and any necessary materials or resources. By setting them up for success, you increase the likelihood of a productive day for both the substitute and your students.

To ensure a seamless transition for the substitute teacher, it is essential to have key information readily available. This may include a seating plan, student profiles highlighting any special needs or behavioural considerations, and emergency procedures, some of this may be given to the sub by the teacher in charge of cover. By arming the substitute with this information, you enable them to step into your role more effectively and maintain continuity in the learning environment, you do this by setting appropriate cover work.

Cover work cannot be written on a crumpled piece of paper at the back of your planner 5 minutes before the end of the day. It is important that as the teacher you communicate as clear of expectations as possible.

Communicating clear expectations to the substitute teacher is crucial in maintaining consistency in your absence. Clearly outline what is expected in terms of behaviour management, lesson delivery, and any specific tasks that need to be completed. By setting clear expectations from the outset, you provide the substitute with a roadmap for success and minimise disruptions during your absence, all of this can be conveyed through a detailed lesson plan, outlining what stage each class is currently at and what stage you would like them to get to by the end of the period.

Building a collaborative relationship with substitute teachers can also enhance their effectiveness in managing your classroom. By establishing open lines of communication and offering support as needed, you create a positive working environment that benefits both the substitute and your students. Encouraging feedback and reflection after their time in your classroom can also help improve future experiences for substitutes covering your classes. It does no harm to catch up with the sub the next time they are in the school and ask how they got on. Often you may find that subs leave notes on your desk for you about particular classes or pupils behaviour or work ethic.

When setting cover, I make sure that my cover work is communicated as clearly as possible, so that there aren't any breakdowns, in communication or by the sub! I find the best way to do this is in tabular form, as shown below.

Period	Class	Work
1	Year 9	...
2		
3	Year 8	...
4	Year 14	...
5		
6	LUNCH	LUNCH
7	Year 10	...
8		
9	Year 12	...

By putting my cover work in tabular form, it can be easily interpreted by whomever is covering. Not only this but it can be easily organised with a printed copy attached to my desk and a digital copy emailed to the teacher in charge of cover or to 'all staff'

By 'weaponising' a substitute teacher through thorough preparation, clear communication, and ongoing support, you can maximise the chances of a successful day in your absence. Empowering substitutes to step into your role seamlessly not only benefit them but also ensures that your students continue to learn and thrive even when you are not present.

It also means you won't have any large-scale tidying to do upon your return.

Lunch

Chapter 59

'It can be lonely' — Mr S

As a Technology and Design teacher, I can say I'm rather fortunate. My specific subject allows me to be quite sociable, through no other reason other than the physical placement of the classrooms and workshops. In a Technology department, it is often the case that you can get anywhere, without walking through a workshop, planning room or office to get there. As a result, you tend to cross paths with other teachers, technicians and students fairly often.

However, with other subjects that's not always the case. I was made aware of a teacher, who taught English, her classroom was located, not in the English department, but in a separate annex build of the school with the music department. Now this isn't the end of the world, as a matter of fact it's quite a common occurrence in overcrowded schools– however it does mean that often, these teachers only interactions in the day are with pupils, and ultimately as a result of the lack of adult interaction, it can be lonely.

Educators spend the majority of their day surrounded by students, teaching multiple classes back-to-back without much time for adult interaction. This constant exposure to pupils can lead to a sense of isolation from other adults, contributing to the loneliness that some teachers experience.

Teachers typically have a packed schedule, seeing students for 9 or 10 periods a day, with minimal breaks in between. In addition, many teachers use their lunch and break times to catch up on work rather than socialise with colleagues. This lack of adult interaction can make teachers feel disconnected and lonely, as they have limited opportunities to engage in meaningful conversations with their peers.

Another factor that can contribute to the loneliness of teaching is the presence of cliques within schools. Just like in any other workplace, schools can have established social groups that may be challenging to penetrate for new or different teachers. If a teacher doesn't fit into these cliques or struggles to find common ground with colleagues, they may feel isolated and lonely within the school community.

Despite the potential for loneliness in teaching, there are ways to combat these feelings and foster a sense of connection and support.

The first of which is, engaging in professional development workshops, conferences, or seminars can provide teachers with opportunities to connect with other educators outside of their immediate school environment. This is a great opportunity for you to not only build a network of teachers in similar situations or subjects as yourself but also will allow you to build a relationship with them and establish a rapport that can be developed upon.

Online forums, local teacher associations, or school-based support groups are another great way of indirectly socialising. They can offer teachers a platform to share experiences, seek advice, and build relationships with like-minded professionals.

On a more personal level it is important to make sure that you take time for yourself both mentally and physically. Taking care of one's physical and mental well-being is crucial in combating loneliness. Teachers should make time for activities they enjoy outside of work, practice self-care routines, and seek support from friends and family members. We often can get bogged down in the day-to-day comings and goings of school life; it is important to make time for those other things in our lives that matter.

By actively seeking out opportunities for connection, building relationships with colleagues, and prioritising self-care, teachers can navigate the potential loneliness that comes with the profession and create a more supportive and fulfilling work environment for themselves.

Chapter 60

'Make friends with your enemy' — Miss W

'Make friends with your enemy' sounds a bit dramatic, doesn't it? Especially when you consider a school setting. Surely no one is your enemy and surely even if there was someone who was your enemy, you shouldn't be expected to have to make friends with them, right?

Well, in the educational setting, your 'enemy' could be interpreted in various ways – it could be a fellow teacher with whom you have conflicting teaching styles, personalities or even, God forbid, you sat in their seat at lunch time. A student who challenges your authority or disrupts the class dynamic, or even a parent who is overly critical or unsupportive of your teaching methods.

Whoever has scorned you enough for you to deem them your enemy, to make friends with them, does not literally mean that. The notion that one is to 'make friends with your enemy' refers to the idea that rather than challenging those who oppose you one way or another, you more choose to adopt a more passive approach to avoid confrontation, this way you enable yourself to achieve another equally dramatic quote of 'Keep you friends close and your enemies closer', you can keep those people closer to you and monitor their actions as opposed to kicking up a fuss.

When it comes to befriending a fellow teacher who may be seen as an adversary, it's essential to remember that collaboration and teamwork are key components of a successful educational environment and are ultimately what the higher powers within a school are focused on. By taking the initiative to build a positive relationship with this colleague, you can create a more harmonious working atmosphere that benefits not only yourselves but also the students you both teach. For example, offering to share resources, seeking their input on lesson planning, or simply engaging in friendly conversations can help bridge any divides and foster mutual respect.

In the context of befriending a challenging student, it's crucial to approach the situation with empathy and understanding. Rather than viewing the student as an opponent, consider them as someone who may be struggling for various reasons. Taking the time to listen to their concerns, offering support and guidance, and showing genuine interest in their well-being can go a long way in transforming the dynamic between you and the student. By building a positive rapport with such students, you not only create a more inclusive classroom environment but also potentially make a lasting impact on their academic and personal growth.

Building friendships with parents who may initially seem like adversaries can also be incredibly beneficial, especially if you plan on staying in your school for a sustained period and will have encounters with them more often than not. Parents play a crucial role in supporting their child's education, and by establishing positive relationships with them, you can enhance communication, trust, and cooperation. This can involve regular updates on their child's progress, soliciting feedback on your teaching methods, and involving them in decision-making processes related to their child's education. By trying to connect with parents on a personal level, you demonstrate your commitment to their child's success and foster a sense of partnership that benefits everyone involved.

Making friends with your 'enemies' as a teacher involves embracing empathy, communication, and collaboration across different facets of the educational landscape. By approaching fellow teachers, students, and parents with an open mind and a willingness to build positive relationships, you can create a more supportive and enriching learning environment for all.

Chapter 61

'Social Media' — Mr B

Over 5.3 billion people use social media, that's a massive 63.8% of the world! Social media has become an integral part of modern society, influencing various aspects of our lives, including education. As a teacher, social media can serve as both your best friend and worst nightmare, offering numerous benefits while also presenting challenges.

One of the significant advantages of social media for teachers is the easy access to a vast array of educational resources. Platforms like Facebook, Twitter, and Instagram host pages and groups dedicated to sharing teaching materials, lesson plans, and innovative teaching strategies. These resources can be invaluable in enhancing classroom instruction and professional development, especially for that of a baby teacher! Not to mention the fact that there are many groups, particularly on Facebook dedicated to sub teachers, subject specific teachers and even a country-based page for every sort of teacher.

Moreover, social media provides a convenient way for teachers to stay up to date with school messages and announcements. Many educational institutions utilise social media platforms to communicate important information to staff, students, and parents promptly. By following official school accounts or joining relevant groups, teachers can ensure they are well-informed about school events, policy changes, and other updates. This is particularly useful for keep an eye on days such as snow days! The last thing you would want is to struggle your way to school and find out it is shut because of the snow.

Additionally, social media enables teachers to build a robust communication network with colleagues from around the world. Through online communities and professional networks, educators can collaborate, share ideas, seek advice, and engage in meaningful discussions on pedagogy and educational trends. This networking opportunity fosters continuous learning and growth within the teaching profession.

On the flip side, having a social media presence as a teacher can also pose significant challenges. One of the primary concerns is privacy invasion and maintaining a professional image online. Teachers are public figures in their communities, and students or parents may attempt to search for them on social media platforms.

This accessibility can lead to unwanted scrutiny of teachers' personal lives or past behaviours: – that one photo of you from fifteen years ago will always crop up if you look hard enough! Students may stumble upon inappropriate content or interactions on a teacher's profile, which could tarnish their reputation or raise questions about their suitability as an educator. This could be as simple as you robotically sharing a post that you never thought twice about, despite the fact it is your own personal preferences, it could be misconstrued as unprofessional, especially considering we live in such a divisive time. Even harmless posts or photos taken out of context can be misconstrued and cause unnecessary controversy.

To mitigate these risks, many teachers opt to adjust their social media settings to private or limit their online presence under pseudonyms or alternate identities. By controlling who can view their posts and information, educators can safeguard their privacy and maintain a professional boundary between their personal and professional lives.

Social media offers valuable opportunities for teachers to access resources, stay informed, and connect with peers but also presents challenges related to privacy and maintaining a professional image. By leveraging the benefits of social media while implementing appropriate privacy measures, educators can navigate this digital landscape effectively.

Chapter 62

'Sharing lifts' — Miss K

At the moment, unless you are a needlessly rich multi-millionaire, you may be aware that there is a cost-of-living crisis going on. A crisis that has been affecting countries worth of people in massively deprecating ways, to the point where people are genuinely struggling. One way in which people are struggling the most is through the cost of fuel, this is something that we can't do without, however it is something we could be doing without.

As a result, a solution to this is to share lifts with other members of staff going your direction. This not only means you would be saving on fuel, potentially halving your monthly bill if you took it in turns to drive week about, but also has numerous other advantages as well.

Sharing a lift with someone can be a great way to build relationships and get to know people better. This can be especially beneficial for teachers, as building positive relationships with colleagues is an important part of the job. By sharing a lift, you have the opportunity to engage in meaningful conversations and connect on a deeper level, on topics that aren't limited to 'school talk'

Not only this, but driving can be stressful, especially during rush hour or in heavy traffic. Sharing a lift with someone can help alleviate this stress, as you have someone to talk to and share the burden of driving. This can make your commute more enjoyable and less taxing. Just be sure to pick a good driving buddy, you don't want to make the situation more stressful being in the passenger seat with the reincarnation of Evil Knievel

While saving fuel is certainly a benefit of sharing lifts, it's also worth considering the environmental impact of driving alone. By sharing a lift with someone, you're reducing the number of cars on the road and contributing to a more sustainable transportation system. This is not only good for the environment, but it also sets a positive example for your students and colleagues.

In addition to saving fuel, sharing a lift can also help you save money on other general running of the car. Less millage on the engine and tyres for example, means longer duration before having to service them, by splitting these costs with someone else, you can both save money and make your commute more affordable.

Parker J. Palmer once said, 'Good teaching cannot be reduced to technique; good teaching comes from the identity and integrity of the teacher.' Sharing lifts with others is just one small way that teachers can demonstrate their commitment to building positive relationships, supporting sustainability, and making a positive impact on their community. By taking these small steps, teachers can create a more supportive and engaging learning environment for everyone involved.

Chapter 63

'Help where you can... within reason' – Miss McC

As a teacher eager to make a positive impact and please those around you, it is essential to remember the importance of helping where you can, within reason. It is in a teacher's DNA to want to help people- it is the fundamental purpose of an educator really. This principle extends not only to pupils but also to staff members in the school community. Balancing the desire to assist with the need to set boundaries and prioritise self-care is crucial for maintaining a healthy and sustainable approach to teaching.

When it comes to helping pupils, teachers often find themselves wanting to go above and beyond to support their students. While this enthusiasm is commendable, it is essential to recognise the importance of setting realistic expectations and boundaries. For example, a teacher may feel compelled to offer extra tutoring sessions outside of school hours to struggling students. While this dedication is admirable, it is crucial for the teacher to also prioritise their own well-being and avoid burnout.

In addition to supporting students, teachers may also feel pressure to help their colleagues in various ways. Whether it's covering a class for a sick teacher or volunteering for extracurricular activities, the desire to be helpful can sometimes lead to overextension. It is important for teachers to remember that while collaboration and teamwork are valuable, they must also consider their own workload and capacity before taking on additional responsibilities.

One key aspect of helping where you can, within reason, is learning how to set boundaries effectively. This means being able to say no when necessary and prioritising self-care in order to avoid burnout. By establishing clear boundaries and communicating openly with both students and colleagues, young teachers can ensure that they are providing support in a sustainable way.

The idea of helping where you can, within reason, is essential for teachers who are eager to make a difference in their school communities. By balancing their desire to assist with the need to set boundaries and prioritise self-care, young teachers can cultivate a sustainable approach to teaching that benefits both themselves and those around them.

Chapter 64

'COFFEE' – Mrs B

When I went to university, I had a friend. This friend was late 80% of the time. If we had a 9 am lecture, you could guarantee that they would arrive in probably around quarter past the hour. The reason for it you ask? Coffee. They would spend much of their commute to the university, sitting in a drive through ordering a coffee. I never understood the reason as to why, until I became a teacher. Now every morning I find myself stopping at the local petrol station, buy a cheap and nasty cup of coffee. I even have a loyalty card for the coffee machine...

While your poison mightn't be coffee, as a teacher, each day presents its unique challenges and demands. From early morning lesson planning to managing a classroom full of energetic students, the role of an educator can be both rewarding and exhausting.

In order to navigate through the daily grind of teaching, it is essential for teachers to find what fuels them and keeps them going throughout the day.

As I've already said for many teachers, coffee is the go-to fuel that kickstarts their day. The aroma of freshly brewed coffee wafting through the air can signal the beginning of a new day filled with possibilities. The caffeine boost from a steaming cup of coffee can provide the much-needed energy to tackle lesson preparations, marking tests, and engage with students effectively. Whether it's a strong espresso shot or a creamy latte, coffee has become synonymous with the teaching profession for its ability to keep teachers alert and focused.

However, some people- I don't know how, don't drink caffeine... however there is other fixes they can have, in today's digital age, podcasts have emerged as a popular source of information and entertainment. For some teachers, listening to a podcast during their morning commute to school can be a refreshing way to start the day. Whether it's an educational podcast that offers teaching tips and strategies or a light-hearted show that brings a smile to their face, podcasts can serve as a source of inspiration and motivation for educators. The power of words spoken by passionate hosts can uplift spirits and set a positive tone for the day ahead.

While it might not be the healthiest option, another way in which other people can find their happy place before or after they come to school is indulging in a breakfast bap dripping with grease can be a guilty pleasure for some teachers. The savoury combination of crispy bacon, melted cheese, and fluffy eggs sandwiched between two warm buns and a of course tomato ketchup, can provide comfort and satisfaction in the early hours of the morning. Despite its calorie-laden nature, a hearty breakfast bap can serve as a comforting ritual that helps teachers gear up for the challenges that lie ahead in the classroom. I may have been hungry writing this part of the chapter...

Apart from coffee, podcasts, and breakfast baps, there are numerous other ways in which teachers can find their daily fuel. Some educators find solace in practicing mindfulness or yoga before starting their day, while others prefer to listen to energising music that pumps them up for teaching. Taking short breaks throughout the day to enjoy a healthy snack or engage in brief physical activity can also help teachers recharge and stay focused during long teaching hours. On a personal level, I enjoy working towards getting my steps in on a daily basis.

Finding what gets you through the day as a teacher is essential for maintaining your well-being and effectiveness in the classroom. Whether it's savouring a cup of coffee, tuning into a podcast, indulging in a breakfast treat, or exploring other sources of daily fuel, prioritising self-care and finding moments of joy amidst the demands of teaching is crucial for long-term success in education.

Chapter 65

'Make the most of your school holidays' — Mr G

As a teacher, the summer holidays offer a much-needed break from the demands of the classroom. When it comes to the last day of term in the summer, the last bell of the day can't come soon enough. As it goes, you think 'happy days! Summer!' However, these long holidays can also fly by quickly, leaving many educators feeling like they didn't make the most of their time off. However, there are ways to capitalise on this time off.

The first few weeks of summer should be dedicated to rest and relaxation. Catch up on sleep, read books for pleasure, and engage in hobbies that you don't have time for during the school year. This will help you feel rejuvenated and ready to tackle the upcoming school year. It's a good opportunity to try out new hobbies and invest time into your own search of new skills and interests.

There is also an opportunity to use some of your summer break to further your professional development. Attend workshops, conferences, or online courses to learn new teaching strategies or expand your knowledge in your subject area. This will not only benefit you but also your students when you return to the classroom. While a lot of in person courses and qualifications don't run in the summer, similar to that of school– there is plentiful opportunity online to prevail of courses and professional development opportunities.

While it may seem counterintuitive to think about work during your summer off, taking some time to plan for the upcoming school year can help reduce stress and anxiety when school starts back up. Create lesson plans, organise your classroom, and set professional goals for the year ahead.

The summer is also the perfect time to explore new places and cultures. Whether you take a trip overseas or explore a nearby city, traveling can broaden your horizons and provide new experiences that can be incorporated into your teaching. If you are a person who is interested in travelling during your time off. make the most of the far away deals and ask your principal for the 'key dates' sheet that they make at the start of every year. This will highlight the dates in which the school are officially taking off and which they are closed by expect staff in to partake in staff development days, from that you then go on to a holiday search sight and book to your hearts content within these dates.

Another more spiritually beneficial way of making the most of your time during summer is, giving back to your community can be a rewarding way to spend your summer holiday. Volunteer at a local charity, mentor a student, or participate in a community service project. This will not only benefit others but also provide a sense of fulfilment and purpose.

Probably most paramount of all however is spending time with family. The summer is a great time to reconnect with loved ones. Plan trips, host barbecues, or simply spend quality time together. Building strong relationships can provide support and motivation throughout the school year.

As educational psychologist and author Jennifer Louden says, 'The trick is to allow yourself time to rest deeply so that you can work, play, love, and create with a renewed sense of energy and passion.' By incorporating these strategies into your summer holiday plans, you can make the most of your time off and return to the classroom feeling refreshed, motivated, and ready to tackle the challenges of the upcoming school year.

Chapter 66

'Don't Sh*t on your doorstep' — Mr L

The concept of 'not sh*tting on your doorstep' in a minefield of red tape and consequences and it can often be misconstrued in multitude of different ways. However, in teaching it refers to being mindful of the potential consequences of mixing one's personal and professional life. Specifically, it involves avoiding actions or behaviours that could negatively impact one's job or relationships with colleagues, students, or parents.

While it is generally acceptable to bring some aspects of one's personal life into the professional sphere, it is important to exercise caution and discretion. This is because personal relationships and issues can sometimes spill over into the workplace, potentially leading to conflicts, misunderstandings, or uncomfortable situations. Afterall, first and foremost, you are being paid to be a professional teacher, and if you can neither be professional nor teach as a result of a past indiscretion with a personal relationship that has spilled into the workplace, then there is a massive cause for concern and senior management or even the board of governors are sure to take note.

One area where this issue can arise is in romantic relationships between teachers and other school staff members. While it is not uncommon for romantic relationships to develop in the workplace, in fact there are many examples I can think of where couples have met in the school setting and are still going strong to this day. It has become a bit of a thing in my school, where many couples have met from working together. Leading many to assume there is something in the water. Regardless of this however, it is important for teachers to consider the potential implications of such relationships, particularly if they end badly. For example, if a teacher is involved in a romantic relationship with another staff member and the relationship ends, they may still have to work together in a professional capacity. This can create tension and make it difficult to maintain a positive and productive working environment.

Further to this, and it goes without saying, romantic relationships between teachers and students are strictly prohibited in all educational institutions due to ethical concerns and power dynamics. Such relationships can lead to allegations of sexual misconduct, which can result in severe consequences for the teacher, including loss of registration, damage to reputation, and even criminal charges.

As a teacher, we are told at university to establish clear boundaries between one's personal and professional life. This may involve keeping personal issues private, avoiding romantic relationships with colleagues or students, and being mindful of how one's behaviour may be perceived by others. Additionally, it is important to always maintain a high level of professionalism and integrity, even outside of the classroom or school setting.

The idea of 'not sh*tting on your doorstep' as a teacher involves being aware of the potential consequences of mixing personal and professional life. While it is acceptable to bring some aspects of one's personal life into the workplace, teachers should exercise caution and discretion to avoid conflicts, misunderstandings, or uncomfortable situations. By establishing clear boundaries and maintaining a high level of professionalism, teachers can minimise the risk of negative consequences and ensure a positive and productive working environment for themselves and their colleagues.

Chapter 67

'Join online support groups' – Miss M

As another chapter has addressed, when you first start the school year, even if it isn't your first, it is absolutely bedlam, people running all over the place trying to get established, set up and prepared for the wave of pupils coming to the school in a few days. You need to be on your game in that moment, so it would be understandable if you come into a school, it's your first day and you take a step back and see everyone running all over the place mad doing what they need to do, and you get forgotten about almost– it is nothing personal. However, there's no doubt, it's a daunting time, and to feel a lack of support is bound to be difficult. However, what I didn't learn until later on in my first year, is that there is support available to you outside of the confines of you school environment.

In the modern age of technology, teachers should take advantage opportunity to connect with colleagues from around the world through online support groups. These virtual communities provide a platform for educators to share resources, seek advice, and collaborate on various educational topics.

Online support groups offer teachers a chance to engage in continuous professional development. By interacting with educators from diverse backgrounds, teachers can gain new perspectives, learn about innovative teaching methods, and stay updated on the latest trends in education.

Not only this but, another significant advantage of online support groups is the ability to share resources. Teachers can exchange lesson plans, teaching materials, and classroom management strategies, which can save time and enhance the quality of their teaching. Using these platforms can allow you to break the mould of your idea of what a resource can be, and allow you to see others with good ideas and develop from that

Online support groups also allow teachers to expand their professional network beyond their immediate surroundings. Building connections with educators worldwide can lead to new collaborations, job opportunities, and friendships.

What I have found also that is a benefit with these groups is the emotional support that is available. Teaching can be a challenging profession, and having a supportive community can make a significant difference. Online support groups provide a space for teachers to vent frustrations, seek advice during tough times, and celebrate successes with like-minded individuals.

However, there are also significant reasons as to why support groups aren't ideal. Engaging in online support groups can be time-consuming. Teachers may find themselves spending excessive amounts of time scrolling through discussions or responding to posts, which could detract from their work-life balance.

You are also cursed by the nature of how vast the network is. Not all information shared in online support groups is accurate or reliable, as a result of the fact that there are members from all over the globe within, all of which comes from different governing bodies who have different defined specifications and criteria that has to be met. Teachers need to critically evaluate the resources and advice they receive to ensure they are implementing best practices in their classrooms.

Undoubtedly so however, you are inevitably destined to fall into, disagreements and conflicts can arise among members with differing opinions or approaches to teaching. Managing these conflicts effectively requires strong communication skills and emotional intelligence.

While there is no doubt that joining online support groups can bring immense value to teachers in terms of professional growth, resource sharing, networking, and emotional support, it is essential to be mindful of the potential drawbacks such as time management challenges, quality of information shared, and potential conflicts within the community.

Chapter 68

'No need to reinvent the wheel, use your support network' – Mr S

It is essential to recognise that there is no need to reinvent the wheel when it comes to creating resources for your classroom. Instead of starting from scratch every time you need a new lesson plan or activity, you can tap into the wealth of knowledge and experience that exists within your support network. This network can include colleagues at your school, online support groups, and resource sharing sites.

One of the most valuable resources available to teachers is their colleagues within the school. These are individuals who have first-hand experience in the same environment and often have a treasure trove of materials and ideas that they are willing to share. By collaborating with other teachers, you can benefit from their expertise and save yourself time and effort by building upon what has already been proven effective.

For example, imagine you are a new science teacher preparing a unit on photosynthesis. Instead of starting from scratch, you could reach out to a more experienced colleague who may have engaging lesson plans, worksheets, and hands-on activities that they have used successfully in the past. By leveraging their resources, you can enhance your own teaching without having to create everything from scratch.

In addition to in-person support at your school, the internet offers a vast array of online support groups and resource sharing sites specifically designed for educators. Platforms like Teachers Pay Teachers, Pinterest, and various Facebook groups provide teachers with access to a plethora of resources created by educators from around the world.

These online communities allow teachers to share lesson plans, worksheets, classroom management strategies, and more. By tapping into these resources, you can benefit from the collective wisdom of a global network of educators who have already developed high-quality materials for almost any topic or grade level.

While utilising existing resources can save time and effort, there is also value in creating your own materials tailored to the specific needs of your students. As educator Rita Pierson once said, 'Every child deserves a champion – an adult who will never give up on them, who understands the power of connection and insists that they become the best that they can possibly be.'

By creating your own resources, you have the opportunity to personalise you're teaching to meet the unique needs and interests of your students. While online resources can be incredibly helpful, they may not always align perfectly with your teaching style or the specific goals you have for your class. Therefore, creating your own materials allows you to tailor them precisely to achieve the outcomes you desire.

As a teacher, it is essential to leverage your support network both in school and online to access existing resources that can enhance your teaching practice. While utilising resources created by others can save time and provide valuable insights, there is also merit in crafting your own materials to meet the individual needs of your students.

Chapter 69

'Emotional drainers and radiators'– Miss C

As a teacher, you spend a significant amount of time interacting with students, colleagues, and parents. These interactions can be incredibly rewarding, but they can also be emotionally draining.

First, let's define what I mean by emotional drainers and radiators. Emotional drainers are people who tend to bring us down emotionally. They may be negative, critical, or pessimistic, and their behaviour can leave us feeling exhausted and depleted. On the other hand, emotional radiators are people who uplift and energise us. They are positive, supportive, and optimistic, and their presence can help us feel more motivated and engaged.

It's important to note that everyone has the potential to be both an emotional drainer and a radiator at different times. Our moods and behaviours can fluctuate based on a variety of factors, including our own emotional state, stress levels, and life circumstances. However, some people tend to be more consistently draining or radiating than others.

So why is it important for teachers to be aware of emotional drainers and radiators? As a teacher, you are in a position of influence. You can shape the emotional climate of your classroom and school community. When you surround yourself with positive people, you create a more supportive and uplifting environment for yourself and your students. On the other hand, when you spend time with negative people, you may find that your own energy and motivation begin to wane.

Pay attention to how you feel after interacting with different people. Do you feel energised and inspired, or drained and depleted? This can be a good indicator of whether someone is a radiator or a drainer.

Observe the behaviour of the people around you. Do they tend to focus on the positive aspects of a situation, or the negative? Do they offer support and encouragement, or criticism and negativity?

Consider the impact that different people have on your mood and motivation. Do certain people leave you feeling more positive and engaged, while others bring you down?

Set boundaries with emotional drainers. It's okay to limit your interactions with people who consistently bring you down. You may need to establish clear boundaries around your time and energy in order to protect yourself from their negative influence.

Seek out emotional radiators. Surrounding yourself with positive people can help boost your own mood and motivation. Look for opportunities to connect with colleagues, friends, and family members who uplift and inspire you.

As a teacher, it's important to prioritise your own emotional well-being. By being aware of emotional drainers and radiators in your life, you can take steps to protect yourself from negativity and surround yourself with positivity. This can help you create a more supportive and uplifting classroom environment for yourself and your students.

Period 7

Chapter 70

'LSAs and support technicians'– Mr J

As a technology and design teacher, my daily lesson planning isn't as conventional as you would expect. As well as ensuring I have my booklets, work and resources set out ready for each lesson– I also need to make sure that I have the materials ready for the practical aspect of the lesson as well.

This usually means having wood cut to length, toolboxes ready and the workshop tidy. You may be wondering how I find the time to do all of this– well that's simple, my technician. He is a fantastically gifted man who knows more about woodwork, metalwork and general bodgery than I ever could even begin to know. You never need to ask him, 'can you get this ready for period 2?', he already has it ready to go. He easily is responsible for the seamless transition from theory work in the classroom to the practical work in the workshop. A true linchpin in the department.

However, that being said it isn't just technicians that need to be recognised. A school has many multi-facetted roles, encompassed by a wide range of people. Some roles of which are no more important than LSAs, Learning support assistants.

In any educational institution, the smooth functioning and success of daily operations rely heavily on the collaborative efforts of various staff members. Among these important roles are Learning Support Assistants (LSAs) and department-specific technicians, such as those in technology, science, or home economics departments.

It is crucial to recognise and appreciate the invaluable contributions these individuals make to the overall learning environment within a school.

LSAs play a vital role in supporting student learning by providing additional assistance to students who may require extra help in understanding concepts or completing tasks. They work closely with teachers to implement individualised education plans for students with special needs, ensuring that each student receives the necessary support to reach their full potential.

For example, an LSA may work one-on-one with a student who has dyslexia to help them improve their reading skills or assist a student with autism in developing social communication skills.

Department technicians, on the other hand, are instrumental in maintaining the essential infrastructure that supports teaching and learning within specific departments. For instance, a technology technician ensures that all machinery equipment is functioning properly, allowing teachers to integrate practicality seamlessly into their lessons. In a science department, technicians prepare lab materials and equipment, enabling students to engage in hands-on experiments safely and effectively. Higher education technicians provide critical support for research projects and academic programs, contributing to the overall success of the institution.

Recognising the roles of LSAs and department technicians is essential for fostering a supportive school environment where all staff members feel valued and respected for their contributions.

By acknowledging the expertise and dedication of these individuals, schools can promote collaboration among different departments and create a culture of mutual respect and appreciation. This collaborative approach not only enhances the overall efficiency of school operations but also enriches the educational experience for both students and staff.

LSAs and department technicians play integral roles in ensuring the smooth functioning of schools and supporting student learning across various subjects. By recognising and appreciating the contributions of these individuals, educational institutions can create a more inclusive and supportive environment that benefits everyone involved in the learning process.

In saying all of this, it is important to take time to acknowledge these individuals. Simply, by saying 'Thank you' at the end of a lesson, or potentially gifting them a small gift at Christmas or the end of the year, just to show your appreciation to them.

At the end of the day, the adage of 'do on to others as you would want to do on to you' is very important here. Try your best to be empathetic and understand of others and put yourself in their shoes, imagine how you would feel if you were handed a nice wee, 'just because' present at the start of the day or end of the term. It really does go a long way.

Chapter 71

'Manage your time well'– Mrs K

I can near enough guarantee, the large majority of teachers do the same thing every year as soon as they get their timetable. They look at the position of the classes and also look at where all the free periods, and we all do it. We all look at those free periods and think 'happy days! That period there I'll be able to do X,Y,Z in that time!'. The real reality of teaching is unless you are well prepared, you never end up using your free periods in the way you initially set out to do.

Time is a valuable resource in any regard, however none more so than with teaching. With the many responsibilities that come with the job, it is crucial to make the most of every minute available. One such opportunity for maximising productivity is during free periods. These periods, often scattered throughout the week, can provide teachers with valuable time to catch up on work, plan lessons, or collaborate with colleagues. However, without proper planning and utilisation, these periods can quickly slip away, leaving teachers feeling overwhelmed and unprepared.

The first step in effectively utilising free periods is to have a clear understanding of their purpose. Free periods are not simply a break from teaching, although often they are used as such; they are an opportunity to catch up on tasks that may have been overlooked during busy class hours. This might include marking coursework, preparing materials for upcoming lessons, or meeting with students for extra help. By recognising the potential of these periods, teachers can begin to approach them with a sense of purpose and intentionality.

One common challenge that teachers face during free periods is distractions. With the freedom to use this time as they see fit, it can be easy to become side-tracked by non-work-related tasks. To combat this, it's important to establish clear boundaries and prioritise tasks. Creating a to-do list at the beginning of each week can help teachers stay focused and ensure that they are making progress on important tasks. Additionally, setting aside specific times for checking emails or social media can help minimize distractions during free periods.

Another important aspect of utilising free periods is being prepared. This means having all necessary materials and resources readily available. For example, having access to a computer or laptop can make it easier to complete tasks such as marking or creating lesson plans. Additionally, keeping a well-organised workspace can help teachers quickly locate materials and resources needed during their free period. By being prepared and having the necessary tools at hand, teachers can maximise their productivity during these valuable periods.

Collaboration with other teachers is another way that teachers can utilise their free periods. By working together, teachers can share ideas, resources, and strategies for improving student outcomes. This might include co-planning lessons or discussing effective teaching methods. Additionally, free periods can provide an opportunity for teachers to seek feedback and support from their colleagues. By fostering a collaborative environment, teachers can create a stronger sense of community and improve overall job satisfaction.

In addition to collaboration, free periods can also provide an opportunity for self-care and reflection.

Teaching can be a demanding profession both physically and emotionally. Taking time during free periods to recharge and refocus can help teachers maintain their energy and enthusiasm throughout the day. This might include taking a short walk, practicing mindfulness or meditation, or simply taking a few moments to relax and recharge. By prioritising self-care, teachers can improve their overall well-being and better serve their students.

It's also important for teachers to recognise that not all tasks are created equal. Some tasks may be more pressing or time-sensitive than others. By prioritising tasks based on urgency and importance, teachers can ensure that they are making the most of their free periods. For example, marking may take priority over planning future lessons if there is an upcoming deadline for report cards. By recognising these priorities, teachers can allocate their time accordingly and avoid feeling overwhelmed by less important tasks.

Finally, it's important for teachers to remember that free periods are not just about getting caught up on work; they are also an opportunity for growth and development. This might include attending professional development workshops or engaging in online learning opportunities during free periods. By investing in their own professional growth, teachers can improve their skills and knowledge base, ultimately benefiting their students in the long run.

Effectively utilising free periods as a teacher is essential for maximising productivity and staying prepared for the demands of the job. By recognising the potential of these periods, setting clear boundaries and priorities, being prepared with necessary materials and resources, collaborating with colleagues, prioritising self-care and reflection, recognising task priorities based on urgency and importance, and investing in professional growth and development, teachers can make the most of this valuable time and better serve their students' needs.

Chapter 72

'Try and find a department with others in it'– Mr R

Finding a department in a school with people in it is crucial for teachers as it provides them with a supportive network, opportunities for collaboration, and a platform for continuous learning and growth. Teaching can be a challenging profession, and having colleagues to bounce ideas off can significantly enhance one's teaching practice. When teachers work in isolation, they may struggle to find their footing and navigate the complexities of the education system. Being part of a department allows teachers to share resources, strategies, and experiences, ultimately benefiting both the teachers and their students.

One of the best advantages of being part of a department is the built-in support system it offers. Teaching can be emotionally taxing, and having colleagues who understand the challenges can provide much-needed encouragement and advice. Your department is the front line in dealing with the ups and down of school life. First and foremost, at the end of the day, these are the people whom you can share stories, quips and funny anecdotes from at breaktime and lunch time. Having no one to do that may result in there being a lonely experience.

Collaboration among teachers within a department can lead to innovative teaching practices and improved student outcomes. When teachers work together on lesson planning, assessments, or extracurricular activities, they can leverage each other's strengths and expertise. This collaborative environment fosters creativity and professional growth. The best of departments are the departments in which they have a well-functioning group of teachers within, these teachers are good at communicating, organising and arranging between each other.

Teaching is a dynamic profession that requires continuous learning and adaptation to new pedagogical approaches. By being part of a department with experienced educators, new teachers can benefit from mentorship and guidance. Henry Ford encapsulates this best, 'Coming together is a beginning; keeping together is progress; working together is success.'

Finding a department in a school with people in it is essential for teachers to thrive in their profession. The collaborative environment, support network, and opportunities for continuous learning make being part of a department an enriching experience that benefits both educators and students.

Chapter 73

'Work with SLT'– Mrs M

In the educational setting, collaborating with senior leader teachers can be a strategic approach to problem-solving within a department or year group. Rather than immediately escalating issues to the vice principal or principal, seeking guidance and support from experienced colleagues can offer several advantages.

Senior leader teachers often possess a wealth of experience and knowledge accumulated over years of teaching. By engaging with them, you tap into a valuable resource within your school community. These individuals have likely encountered similar challenges in the past and can provide insights, strategies, and best practices to address the issue at hand. Moreover, forming strong relationships with senior leaders fosters a sense of camaraderie and collaboration within the teaching staff, creating a supportive network that can enhance professional growth and development.

Senior leader teachers typically hold leadership positions within the school and have demonstrated excellence in their teaching practice. Leveraging their expertise can offer mentorship opportunities for less experienced educators. By working closely with senior leaders, you can benefit from their mentorship, guidance, and feedback on your ideas and approaches to problem-solving. This collaborative process not only helps resolve immediate issues but also contributes to your professional development as an educator.

Seeking assistance from senior leader teachers empowers educators to take ownership of challenges within their department or year group. By actively engaging in problem-solving discussions and seeking input from experienced colleagues, teachers demonstrate initiative, critical thinking skills, and a proactive approach to addressing issues. Presenting solutions rather than problems to the school principals showcases teachers' ability to collaborate effectively, think creatively, and contribute positively to the school community.

Working with senior leader teachers to solve problems cultivates a culture of continuous learning and improvement among educators. Through collaborative problem-solving processes, teachers have the opportunity to exchange ideas, share perspectives, and learn from each other's experiences. This collaborative approach not only leads to effective solutions but also promotes professional growth by expanding knowledge, refining skills, and fostering innovation in teaching practices.

Collaborating with senior leader teachers offers numerous benefits for educators seeking to address challenges within their department or year group. By leveraging the expertise, mentorship, and support of experienced colleagues, teachers can develop effective solutions, enhance professional growth, and demonstrate leadership qualities within the school community.

Chapter 74

'If you want the department- earn it'– Mrs K

As a NQT, it is easy to think you can walk into a school and climb through the ranks easily. I remember a particular person at university, who had the mindset of 'VP by 28'. While it is good to have aspirations and goals, you also have to be very realistic to the real dynamic of how a school works and the structure within.

Unless you are in a school where they think the sun shines from somewhere through your digestive tract, it is unlikely that you will get anything without having to work for it, and by work, I mean work.

This chapter specifically focuses on the idea of earning what you want, as opposed to expecting as a result of your position.

Fundamentally it is important to understand that the idea of earning what you want is a crucial concept that applies to both students and teachers. This idea emphasises the importance of working hard, demonstrating dedication, and proving that you deserve certain positions or responsibilities. For teachers who aspire to become head of department, head of year, senior teacher, vice principal, or even principal, this concept is particularly relevant.

To become a leader in a school setting, one must put in a significant amount of effort and time. This might involve taking on additional responsibilities, pursuing further education or professional development, and consistently demonstrating strong leadership skills. It is not a position that is handed to someone; it must be earned through hard work and dedication. It would be naive for a 'baby teacher' to come into a school and expect to be handed the position of HOD or HOY. Now, while it is not entirely unheard of, it is a slim chance where the opportunity might be given to a NQT so early on in their career.

Once a leadership position has been attained, the work does not stop there. In fact, the expectations and responsibilities may increase. Leaders are expected to uphold high standards and continue to work hard to maintain the reputation and success of the school. They can easily lose their position if they do not meet these expectations. Therefore, it is essential for leaders to remain dedicated and committed to their role, even after they have achieved it.

Very early into my career I was given the responsibly of managing a department in the absence of the head, shortly after I was also given the opportunity at a chance of being in charge of the year 9s within the school. I can speak from personal experience, as a young teacher who doesn't fully know the minutia of the education process, on top of the additional workload- it can be stressful process of which you end up feeling like a hose pinched close with the water continuing to build pressure within.

In addition to hard work and dedication, humility is also an important characteristic for leaders in a school setting. Even after achieving a leadership position, it is essential to remain humble and approachable. This means listening to others, seeking input and feedback, and recognising that there is always room for improvement. By remaining humble, leaders can create a positive and inclusive environment that encourages collaboration and growth.

As John Wooden, a famous American basketball coach, once said, 'Talent is God-given. Be humble. Fame is man-given. Be grateful. Conceit is self-given. Be careful.' Highlighting the importance of remaining humble, even when achieving great success or recognition.

The idea of earning what you want in a school setting is an important concept for teachers who aspire to become leaders- it can be healthy to have such a drive. It involves hard work, dedication, and a commitment to upholding high standards once a leadership position has been attained. Furthermore, humility is an essential characteristic for leaders to embody, as it allows them to create a positive and inclusive environment that encourages collaboration and growth.

Period 8

Chapter 75

'Your free periods- are not yours!'– Miss O

As a teacher, it is essential to be aware of your legal rights when it comes to free periods. These periods are crucial for teachers to plan lessons, mark work, and attend to other administrative tasks, or even tidying. However, the reality is that free periods are often not entirely free as teachers may be called upon to cover another class or assist with other duties during these times.

One key aspect that all educators should be aware of is that they are entitled to a minimum number of free periods as per statutory regulations. These free periods are not just a luxury but a legal right that teachers have to ensure they can fulfil their teaching responsibilities effectively.

However, there is a common misconception among newly qualified teachers (NQTs) that they are entitled to additional free periods on top of the standard minimum requirement. While this may have been the case in the past, various factors such as oversubscription, budget constraints, and understaffing have led to a grey area regarding this statutory requirement.

It is crucial for NQTs to understand that the allocation of additional free periods beyond the minimum requirement is now at the discretion of the school. Due to various challenges faced by educational institutions, including financial constraints and staffing issues, schools may not always be able to provide extra free periods for NQTs. Although often you find that most schools will oblige where possible it is not a right that as a NQT you now have.

It is imperative for all teachers, especially NQTs, to be mindful of their rights regarding free periods. While the statutory requirement for minimum free periods exists, the availability of additional free periods has become a grey area subject to school discretion. By staying informed and advocating for their rights, teachers can ensure they have the necessary time and resources to excel in their roles.

Chapter 76

'Toilet breaks are a precious commodity'– Mr B

As one of the last 'noble professions' out there, you would think as educators, you would be entitled to certain perks, and you are long holidays, every weekend off, or even, ready access to laminators and photocopying... however, one of the perks you can say educators don't get is, readily available access to the bathroom. Unlike many other professions, teachers often have to wait until their scheduled breaks or lunchtime to use the restroom.

The reason for this is the non-stop nature of teaching. From the moment the school day begins, teachers are responsible for managing their classrooms, teaching lessons, and supervising students. This constant demand for attention can make it challenging to take a break, even for something as basic as using the bathroom.

Erin Gruwell, the inspiration behind the film, 'Freedom Writers' once aptly summed up this idea by saying 'As a teacher, you're like a superhero. You have the amazing ability to hold it in for hours on end.'

Preparation is key to managing this challenge, if we can stay prepared, we can overcome this tinkle dilemma. Teachers can take several steps to minimise the impact of limited bathroom breaks on their daily routine. Simply by staying on top photocopying, sending emails and marking, you can reduce the time to do this, taken during your breaks and maximise your free time in your breaks. So that you can go and relieve yourself when you need to.

Fortunately, many teachers find that their colleagues are understanding and supportive when it comes to bathroom breaks. Sharing strategies and experiences can help teachers navigate this challenge and find creative solutions.

'When you gotta go, you gotta go. But as a teacher, you learn to get creative with your timing.' – Anonymous Teacher

While limited bathroom breaks can be a challenge for teachers, preparation and support can help minimise the impact. By planning ahead and working together, teachers can ensure that they are able to meet the needs of their students while also taking care of their own basic needs.

Chapter 77

'You're on a conveyor belt'– Mrs J

In 2018, the Ford Motor company reportedly were producing a staggering 1200 cars a day, that is a car every 1.2 minutes. Isn't that a staggering statistic given the amount of work that goes into assembling a car. Or maybe this is the Technology and Design teacher 'geeking out'.

While teaching isn't exactly as efficient as the largest motor manufacturing companies in the world, it can sometimes feel like a production line.

Teaching is often likened to a production line, where educators find themselves in a continuous cycle of welcoming new students, nurturing them, and eventually sending them off into the world. Just like a production line, teachers must adapt to the unique needs and characteristics of each group of students that come through their classrooms.

In a post-primary school setting, this concept is particularly evident. Consider a high school teacher who teaches a group of first years. Over the course of the five or seven years, these students progress through different levels of education under the guidance of their teachers. Each year, the teacher witnesses growth, challenges, and achievements within their cohort of students.

As the students advance from first years to fifth years, or potentially even through to upper sixth, the teacher plays a crucial role in not only imparting knowledge but also shaping their overall development. The teacher must adjust their teaching strategies, provide individualised support, and foster a positive learning environment to meet the changing needs of each group of students.

At the time of leaving school, these fifth years or upper sixths move on to pursue higher education or enter the workforce, marking the end of their time in that particular teacher's classroom. The teacher then begins anew with a fresh group of first years, restarting the cycle once again. This continuous turnover of students reflects the cyclical nature of teaching, akin to a production line where individuals come and go in regular intervals.

The comparison between teaching and a production line underscores the repetitive yet dynamic nature of educators' roles. Just as products move along an assembly line, students progress through different stages of education with teachers guiding them along the way. Despite the cyclical nature of teaching, each cohort brings new challenges and opportunities for growth, making every cycle unique and rewarding for both teachers and students alike.

Chapter 78

'You're just a number'– Mr McC

In the educational system, teachers play a crucial role in shaping the future of students, as this book has stated so many times over already. However, with that being said, there is a prevalent notion that teachers can sometimes be reduced to just a number within the school environment. This perception can stem from various factors such as standardised testing, administrative pressures, and bureaucratic systems.

One argument supporting the idea that teachers can be seen as just a number within the school is the emphasis on quantitative measures of success. In many educational institutions, teachers are evaluated based on metrics like student test scores or attendance rates for example. This focus on numbers can overshadow the qualitative aspects of teaching, leading to teachers feeling devalued and reduced to mere statistics. We aren't seen for our individual qualities we bring to the classroom or the school, and our contributions are seen in a measurable pass/fail percentage rather than an immeasurable qualitive way. You could be the modern-day incarnation of Mother Teresa, however if your pass mark is plummeting from year to year, being a saint isn't going to do nothing and sooner or later you will be asked to account for these poor results, or even just booted out.

For example, in schools where standardised testing is heavily emphasised, teachers may feel pressured to 'teach to the test' rather than focusing on holistic education. This can result in a narrow curriculum that prioritises exam results over critical thinking skills and creativity.

Not to mention this but, administrative demands and paperwork can also contribute to teachers feeling like they are just a number. The increasing amount of paperwork, data collection, and reporting requirements can take away valuable time and energy from actual teaching and building relationships with students.

However, on the other hand, it is essential to recognise that teachers are not just numbers but individuals with unique talents, passions, and contributions. Effective teaching goes beyond measurable outcomes and encompasses qualities like empathy, creativity, and dedication. Good schools with happy staff understand the significance of this and promote the passion and contributions of staff and make them feel part of the school community.

Teachers have the power to inspire students, ignite curiosity, and instil a love for learning that cannot be quantified by numbers alone. As educator Rita Pierson famously said, 'Every child deserves a champion – an adult who will never give up on them, who understands the power of connection and insists that they become the best that they can possibly be.'

Moreover, strong teacher–student relationships are built on trust, respect, and genuine care. These intangible qualities cannot be captured by standardised tests or performance evaluations but are fundamental to creating a positive learning environment. While there may be instances where teachers feel like they are just a number within the school system, it is crucial to remember that teaching is a deeply human profession that thrives on personal connections and individualised approaches. By valuing teachers as unique individuals with diverse strengths and talents, we can create a more supportive and empowering educational environment for both educators and students.

Chapter 79

'Teaching requires a level of acting'– Dr K

When I was third year of university, I had an observation during teaching practice, it went well thankfully, but the feedback I was given will stick with me for the rest of my life. To be honest with you it never dawned on me at that point, but now that I realised it, it's hard not to see it. It's obvious really.

The lecturer who gave me the feedback was a classically eccentric man. The type of man that wears brogues not oxfords and has a pocket watch to accompany his pin stripped three-piece suit, the man even drove a 'Jaaaaaag' not a jaguar car, one of the old types too. He said that he could see that there was a level of 'acting' with me, as when I teach, its exactly not how I come across normally. He said 'teaching requires a level of acting, and you are a master of all actors'.

He has a point though, as a teacher you do have to act. Teaching is a profession that demands not only knowledge and expertise but also a certain level of performance. Teachers are often required to put on a brave face and act out a role, regardless of their personal struggles or insecurities. This idea of teachers as actors is particularly evident in situations where they must conceal their own emotions and project a sense of confidence and composure for the benefit of their students.

Imagine a scenario where a teacher has just received distressing news before heading into the classroom. Despite feeling overwhelmed with emotions, they must set aside their personal troubles and put on a façade of normalcy for their students. This ability to compartmentalise personal issues and focus on the needs of the students is a crucial aspect of being an effective teacher.

For example, a teacher who has recently experienced a loss in their family must still walk into the classroom with a smile and engage with their students as if nothing is amiss. This act of emotional labour can be mentally taxing, requiring the teacher to suppress their own feelings in order to create a positive learning environment for their students.

Another aspect of the teacher-as-actor concept is the need to exude confidence even in moments of self-doubt. Teachers, like all individuals, may struggle with feelings of inadequacy or imposter syndrome. However, when they step into the classroom, they are expected to embody authority and assurance.

For instance, a new teacher who is still finding their footing in the profession must present themselves as knowledgeable and confident in front of their students. Despite any internal uncertainties, they must deliver lessons with conviction and poise to establish credibility and maintain control over the classroom.

The notion of teachers as actors underscores the performative nature of the teaching profession. Teachers are called upon to mask their personal challenges and insecurities behind a professional facade for the sake of their students' well-being and educational experience.

Chapter 80

'Your life isn't your own as a teacher'– Mr G

As a teacher, the concept of personal freedom takes on a unique meaning. Unlike many other professions, the life of a teacher is not entirely their own. Various aspects of the teaching profession dictate how teachers live their lives, often imposing restrictions and responsibilities that can significantly impact their personal freedom.

Even on a fundamental level, teachers are often judged to the highest standard. Teachers are subject to the same laws as everyone else, but they are often held to a higher standard due to their role in shaping young minds. This means that teachers must adhere to strict codes of conduct both inside and outside the classroom. Regular 'access checks' are conducted to ensure that teachers maintain appropriate behaviour and uphold professional standards at all times. It's not just as simple for a teacher to get drunkenly arrested after a fight in a bar– yes there may not be any ramifications from this altercation, but governing bodies will note this and often deny your clearance as a teacher– if this is the case, it's only a matter of time before your school finds out and then you receive a 'dear John'

One striking way in which a teacher's life is not entirely their own is the constant interaction with students, even outside of school hours. It is not uncommon for teachers to bump into their students while running errands or socialising in their community. This blurring of boundaries between personal and professional life can make it challenging for teachers to fully disconnect from their role. I know of one case where a high-positioned teacher who found herself under scrutiny due to her personal choices outside of school. This long tenured teacher decided to move houses after several instances where she was spotted by students while shopping with wine in her basket. This incident highlighted how even seemingly mundane activities can have repercussions for teachers in terms of public perception and professional reputation.

One of the most common ways in which teachers can have their lives opened up upon against their wills is social media. Teachers must be cautious about their online presence as anything they post on social media can be easily accessed by students, parents, and school administrators. Inappropriate content or controversial opinions shared online can lead to disciplinary actions or damage to one's professional image.

However, hope is not lost– big brother has not won in this case! There are ways to limit this where possible! To prevent these challenges from overwhelming their personal lives, teachers can take proactive steps such as:

- Setting clear boundaries between work and personal time
- Being mindful of their actions in public spaces
- Maintaining professionalism in all interactions, both online and offline

By establishing healthy boundaries and being aware of the unique demands of the teaching profession, educators can navigate the complexities of balancing personal freedom with professional responsibilities more effectively.

Chapter 81

'Sacrifices'– Miss McC

I went to university with a woman who later became an engineer– after the day of graduation, she never taught again, still hasn't. However, she still very much is in our friend circle, a circle of teachers; I am a teacher, her friends are teachers, even her partner is a teacher. This poses logistical issues when it comes to planning for us.

We have a group chat, and on occasions where the stars align, it seems that the wayward ask of, 'drinks tomorrow?' is picking up traction. Things seem good... too good, hope begins to shine through, and I begin to taste the first sip of beer on my lips. Then... 'I can't I'm working'. That dreaded message where in a heartbeat the engineer destroys everything– as they do.

Now, I don't have a hatred to engineers. Not at all... its more, I have a disliking to everyone who doesn't have the same schedule as teachers... which is everyone really.

What has taken me all too long to realise is that as a teacher, there is a certain level of sacrifices to be made, both socially, finically and morally as well.

Being a teacher is a noble profession that comes with its own set of sacrifices, encompassing social, financial, and moral aspects. Teachers often find themselves making sacrifices in various areas of their lives to fulfil their roles effectively.

The demanding nature of the profession often requires teachers to dedicate a significant amount of time and energy to their work, leaving them with limited time for personal relationships and social activities. Teachers may have to forego social events, gatherings, or even family time to meet the demands of their job. This can lead to feelings of isolation or loneliness as they prioritise their students' needs over their own social well-being.

Furthermore, teachers may also face challenges in maintaining friendships outside of work due to the unique stressors and responsibilities that come with being an educator. Engineers, doctors, train drivers or personal trainers all have their own hours to work respectively, however none seem to ever come anywhere near par with a teacher. As a result, it may be often hard to coordinate or even relate to those who you are friends with, the non-teachers. The emotional toll of dealing with students' academic struggles, behavioural issues, or personal challenges can make it difficult for teachers to switch off from work mode and engage fully in social interactions. Often, I find in my close circle of friends, the chat always seems to turn into venting about our schools, pupils or staff- this as a result can isolate those who can't relate to the profession.

Financial sacrifices are another aspect that teachers often have to contend with. Despite the crucial role they play in shaping future generations, teachers are not always compensated adequately for their hard work and dedication. As a teacher it is important to know that unless you can pick 7 lucky numbers it is unlikely that you will ever make your millions teaching. Many teachers struggle with low salaries that may not reflect the level of education, training, and commitment required for the job. Particularly starting out as an NQT, the wages in which you receive are drastically poorer than someone your age working in an equivalent job in a different sector. Teachers may find themselves spending their own money on classroom supplies, resources, or professional development opportunities to enhance their teaching practice. This out-of-pocket spending can further strain their finances and limit their ability to save for the future or enjoy a comfortable lifestyle.

On a moral level, teachers are frequently faced with ethical dilemmas that require them to make difficult decisions that align with their values and principles. They must navigate complex situations involving students, parents, colleagues, and administrators while upholding professional ethics and standards. This can sometimes mean sacrificing personal beliefs or preferences for the greater good of the educational community. Teachers may also encounter moral challenges related to issues such as academic integrity, student discipline, diversity and inclusion, or conflicts of interest. Balancing competing interests and staying true to one's moral compass can be emotionally taxing and demanding for educators.

There is no doubt in my mind that being a teacher entails a multitude of sacrifices across social, financial, and moral dimensions. Despite the challenges and hardships, they face, teachers continue to make invaluable contributions to society by nurturing young minds and shaping the leaders of tomorrow.

Chapter 82

'Actions have consequences'– Mr J

The role of a teacher goes beyond imparting knowledge to students. Teachers are expected to uphold professional standards, abide by legal requirements, and adhere to ethical principles. This chapter explores the consequences of a teacher's actions in relation to their professionalism, the law, and ethics.

When considering teaching, professionalism is crucial in the profession. Teachers must demonstrate competence, dedication, and commitment to their students' learning. They should also exhibit respect, fairness, and integrity in their interactions with colleagues, parents, and students. For instance, a teacher who consistently arrives late to class or fails to prepare lessons may face negative consequences such as decreased student engagement, parent complaints, and potential disciplinary action from school administration. If you are upholding the highest level of professionalism then this will be a non-issue, however often teachers behaviour or habits can result in red flags been noted by management.

Teachers are bound by various laws and policies that govern education. These legal requirements cover areas such as student privacy, special education, discipline, and employment rights. For example, a teacher who discloses confidential student information without proper authorisation could face legal repercussions under the 'Freedom of information act 2000'. Similarly, a teacher who fails to provide appropriate accommodations for a student with a disability could be in violation of the UK Education Healthcare Plan (EHC Plan).

Another way in which teachers may be liable and as a result their actions catching up with them is ethically. Ethical dilemmas can arise in various situations, such as grading, discipline, and confidentiality. Teachers must make decisions based on moral principles and act in the best interests of their students. For example, a teacher who suspects a student is being abused at home may have an ethical obligation to report the situation to the designated head of safeguarding in the school, even if doing so could strain the student–teacher relationship. You, as the teacher have the designated duty of care to anyone under the age of 18 in your classroom at that given time.

While teachers are expected to provide support and guidance to students, there are times when their hands may be tied due to external factors. For instance, if a student requests extra time on a piece of coursework but has not followed proper procedures for receiving accommodations under special education laws, the teacher may be unable to grant the request without risking legal consequences. In another scenario, a teacher may want to advocate for a student facing bullying but lacks concrete evidence, making it difficult to take action without potentially violating the accused student's rights.

Teachers' actions can also have consequences in terms of communication, setting boundaries, and advocating for students. For example, a teacher who fails to communicate clearly with parents about a student's progress may face parental dissatisfaction and potential conflicts. Additionally, a teacher who does not establish appropriate boundaries between themselves and students could face accusations of misconduct or exploitation. Finally, a teacher who advocates too aggressively on behalf of a student might inadvertently create tension within the school community or compromise the student's long-term success.

Teaching involves a delicate balance between professionalism, legal compliance, and moral decision-making. Understanding the potential consequences of one's actions can help educators navigate this complex landscape and provide the best possible learning experience for their students.

Period 9

Chapter 83

'Your niche that you can bring to extra-curricular activities'— Mr B

As a newly qualified teacher stepping into the educational realm, it is crucial to understand the significance of making a lasting impression in a school environment, especially if you are seeking a permanent position. While excelling in your teaching duties is paramount, it is not necessarily always the first thing in which people notice. Going above and beyond by contributing to the school community through extra-curricular activities can truly set you apart.

One effective way to make a mark in a school setting is by identifying a niche where you can offer your unique skills and interests. By finding an area where you can contribute outside of the regular curriculum, you not only showcase your dedication but also demonstrate your commitment to enriching the overall educational experience for students.

For example, if you have a passion for music, you could start a school choir or band, providing students with the opportunity to explore their musical talents. Alternatively, if sports are more your forte, initiating a sports club or coaching a team can help foster teamwork and physical well-being among students.

Engaging in extra-curricular activities not only benefits the students but also allows you to develop relationships with colleagues and showcase your leadership abilities. By taking on responsibilities beyond the classroom, you demonstrate your versatility and willingness to invest in the holistic development of the school community. When I first started in my current school I had a passion for drones, that passion allowed me to purchase a drone through the school and ultimately be able to raise the social media quality of the schools posts by videoing rugby, football and hockey matches, as well as sports day and general promotional footage– this interest made me unique to the school as the only one who could, effectively fly the drone and get quality content.

In the words of renowned educator John Dewey, 'Education is not preparation for life; education is life itself.' Embracing this philosophy, as a newly qualified teacher, immersing yourself in extra-curricular pursuits can significantly enhance your professional growth and leave a lasting impression on those around you.

As you embark on your journey as a newly qualified teacher, remember that making an impression goes beyond just fulfilling your teaching duties. By finding a niche in extra-curricular activities and actively contributing to the school community, you not only showcase your passion and dedication but also position yourself as a valuable asset to the institution. Aspire to be more than just a teacher – be a mentor, a leader, and a source of inspiration for both students and colleagues alike.

Chapter 84

'Connections'– Mr J

A fitting end to this book considering the entire premise of it was a collaborate effort by other teachers, primarily sourced from the connections I have made in my short time in the profession. Without a far stretching range of connections in this sector, I wouldn't be able to achieve the completion of one chapter let alone 84!

As a teacher, building a strong network of connections within the education sector can provide you with a multitude of advantages. These benefits extend beyond the minimum level expected of a teacher and can significantly enhance the teaching and learning experience.

One of the most significant advantages of building a strong network is the ability to share resources with other educators. Teachers are constantly seeking new and innovative ways to engage their students and enhance their learning. By connecting with other educators, you can gain access to a wealth of resources, ideas, and strategies that can help you improve your teaching practices.

For example, by connecting with other teachers on social media platforms or in person through established networking, you can participate in online discussions, share resources, and collaborate on projects. These connections can provide you with a steady stream of new ideas and resources that you can use to improve your teaching practices.

Another advantage of building a strong network is the ability to call upon others for help when needed. Teaching can be a challenging profession, and there may be times when you need advice or support from your colleagues. By building a strong network of connections, you can reach out to other educators who have expertise in specific areas or who have faced similar challenges.

For example, if you are struggling to teach a particular concept or subject, you can reach out to other educators who have experience teaching that subject. They can provide you with guidance, advice, and resources that can help you improve your teaching practices.

This isn't exclusive to other teachers; however, you can call upon the expertise of anyone who might be able to provide relevant expertise to your subject or topic you are teaching. As recently as last year I recruited the expertise of a viral TikTok star who specialises in wood crafts done by hand– while this is a topic and content, I could've taught my Technology classes myself, I found having that culturally relevant star teaching the pupils via 'Zoom' was far more effective than I could've ever had done.

Building a strong network can also provide opportunities for collaboration and professional development. By connecting with other educators, you can engage in collaborative projects, attend professional development workshops and conferences, and participate in online learning communities. These opportunities can help you stay up to date with the latest trends and research in education and improve your teaching practices.

As a good friend once put it, "Building a strong network has been essential to my success as a teacher. By connecting with other educators, I have gained access to a wealth of resources, ideas, and strategies that have helped me improve my teaching practices. I have also been able to call upon my colleagues for help when needed, which has been incredibly valuable."

Building a strong network of connections within the education sector is essential for teachers who want to go above and beyond the minimum level expected. By sharing resources, calling upon others for help, and collaborating on professional development opportunities, teachers can significantly enhance their teaching practices and provide their students with the best possible learning experience.

Printed in Great Britain
by Amazon

48892241R00185